THE BRITISH
HORSE SOCIETY

LEICESTERSHIRE & RUTLAND ON HORSEBACK

AVAILABLE IN THIS SERIES

The Cotswolds on Horseback
Wiltshire on Horseback
Westmorland on Horseback
The Ridgeway Downs on Horseback
Exmoor on Horseback
Somerset on Horseback
Hampshire on Horseback
Leicestershire & Rutland on Horseback

First published 1994
by The British Horse Society
Access & Rights of Way Department
British Equestrian Centre
Stoneleigh Park, Kenilworth
Warwickshire CV8 2LR

A catalogue record for this book is available from the British Library

ISBN 1 899016 04 X

Printed by:
Tripod Press Limited, 7 Wise Street, Leamington Spa, CV31 3AP

Distribution: The British Horse Society, Stoneleigh Park, Kenilworth,
Warwickshire, CV8 2LR

CONTENTS

ACKNOWLEDGEMENTS

A number of people and organisations have given their time and expertise to provide details for this book, or contributed in some other material way.

In particular the British Horse Society would like to thank Anne John, Val Cammock, Joan Loveridge, Vicky Allen, Denise Shaw, John Kilborne, Janice Clarke and Alex Pyper for surveying, developing and describing the routes; Nick Turley for photographs; all members of the Leicestershire County Council Rights of Way Department for their advice, guidance and assistance with the routes; but above all Leicestershire County Council for such generous financial support.

Marcus Bryan '94

Brooke Priory.

FOREWORD

The '.................. on Horseback' series of published rides launched in 1993 has proved extremely popular. This confirms the British Horse Society's belief that many riders need information on routes known to be open, available and providing pleasurable riding.

Many volunteers have worked to research these routes, thus helping to contribute to the Countryside Commission's target of having all rights of way defined, open and signed by the year 2000. This Society wholeheartedly supports this aim which it incorporates into its Access & Rights of Way strategy for the last decade of this Century.

Together with our booklet 'Bed & Breakfast for Horses', these publications enable riders and carriage drivers to plan holidays and other trips. This extends the pleasure and value of owning a horse either to ride or drive, and enables an assortment of different experiences to be enjoyed be they landscape, flora and fauna or historic sites and buildings.

Equestrianism provides one of the most intense pleasures of life, wholly understood only by those who ride, or drive carriages. The Society is proud to contribute in some way to the fulfilment of that pleasure. The challenges of research and development of further routes will continue to be explored.

E A T BONNOR-MAURICE
Chairman, British Horse Society

March 1994

INTRODUCTION

The British Horse Society's ARROW Project aims to identify open and usable routes of varying length and shape (circular, figure-of-eight or linear) to help riders and carriage drivers to enjoy the countryside by means, as far as possible, of the network of public rights of way and the minor vehicular highways. This collection of rides is the result of research and mapping by volunteers who took up the challenge of the ARROW initiative with such enthusiasm and effort.

I am faced with the equally daunting challenge of writing an introductory chapter. Should I write reams about each topic or try simply to point you in the right direction? I have decided upon the second method as the search for information is itself highly educative and stays in the mind better than reading it all in one place. Also, since we all have different expectations of our holiday, a very full guide seemed wrong. Nevertheless, there are a few pointers I would like to suggest to you.

The most important one is to start your planning several months in advance of the trip, including a visit to the area you intend to ride in. You should make endless lists of things to DO (e.g. get the saddle checked) and things to CHECK OUT (can you read a map, for instance). You may find joining the local BHS Endurance Riding Group very helpful, as there you will meet people who can give you information about the degree of fitness needed for yourself and your horse (feeding for fitness not dottiness) , and many other useful hints on adventurous riding. You may also enjoy some of the Pleasure rides organised by the group or by the local Riding Club. These are usually about 15-20 miles and you ride in company, though using a map. You may find them under the title Training Rides. These rides will get both of you used to going into strange country. If you usually ride on well-known tracks, then your horse will find it nerve-racking to go off into new territory, and you yourself may also find the excitement of deep country a bit surprising, so try to widen your experience at home before you go off on holiday.

ACCOMMODATION

Decide how far you wish to ride each day of your holiday, book overnight accommodation for both of you and if possible visit it to see if the five-star suite on offer to your horse is what he is used to. Decide if you want to stable him or to turn him out at the end of the day, and arrange to drop off some food for him, as he will not relish hard work on a diet of green grass, nor will he enjoy a change in his usual food. If you are to have a back-up vehicle, of course, then you will not need to do some of this, but you should certainly make a preliminary visit if you can. The BHS publish a Bed & Breakfast Guide for Horses which is a list of people willing to accommodate horses, and sometimes riders, overnight. The Society does not inspect these places, so you should check everything in advance.

FITNESS

You and your horse should be fit. For both of you , this is a process taking about two months. If you and/or your horse are not in the full flush of youth, then it may take a bit longer. The office chair, the factory floor, or the household duties do not make or keep you fit, but carefully planned exercise will. Remember that no matter how fit your horse seems, he does not keep himself fit - you get him fit. There are several books with details of fitness programmes for a series of rides. Do not forget to build in a rest day during your holiday - neither of you can keep going all the time, day after day. Miles of walking may get you fit, but it uses different muscles from riding; you may get a surprise when you start riding longer distances. It seems to me that the further you intend to ride, the longer your preparation should be. Nothing can be done in a hurry.

Your horse should be obedient, so work on that. If you want him to stand, then he must stand. If you want to go through water, then he must be prepared to walk down a slope or even step down off a bank to go through the stream, so start with puddles and insist that he go through the middle. Does he help you open gates? I hope so, or you will have a great deal of mounting and dismounting to do. Does he tie up - this is essential if you are to have a peaceful pint at lunchtime.

MAPS

Can you read a map? Can you make and read a grid reference (usually referred to as GR)? Get a Pathfinder map of your area and take yourself for a walk and see if you end up where you expect to. Learn to know exactly where you are on the map, and how to understand the symbols (if your map shows hilly ground, the journey will take longer). Can you work out how long a ride is in miles and roughly how long it will take? You will be using rights of way and it is very important that you stay in the line of the path - that is the only place you have a right to be, and you may deviate from that line only as much as is necessary to get you round an obstruction on the path. You are going to be riding over land that forms part of someone's work place and that fact must be respected. It is only by the efforts of farmers and landowners that the countryside exists in its present form - so that we may enjoy it as we pass by.

You will need to know the grid reference (GR.) of the start and end of the various tracks you are to use. Get a copy of an Ordnance Survey (OS) Landranger map and really learn the details on the right-hand side, some of which explain how to arrive at a Grid Reference. Learn to go in the door (Eastings - from left to right) and up the stairs (Northings - from bottom to top). There is a great deal of information on the Landranger maps and not so much on the Pathfinders, but the Pathfinder gives more details on the map itself, so that is the map you will use for the actual ride. Or you may care to buy a Landranger of the area you are visiting and, using a highlighter pen, mark in all the rides you want to make, so that you can see through the marks you make. Then get from any Outdoor shop a map case which will allow you to read the map without taking it out of the case and which you can secure round yourself. Also, you should know if you are facing north, south, east or west as you ride. Quite important if you think about it, as it is no good riding into the sunset if you are meant to be going south. Plastic orienteering compasses are cheap and reliable.

TACK

Have your tack thoroughly checked by your saddler, as there is nothing so annoying as a sore back which could have been prevented, or an unnecessarily broken girth strap. How are you going to carry the essential headcollar and rope each day? What about spare shoes, or a false shoe?

What to take on the ride depends on how

much back-up you have. If you have to carry a change of clothes, etc., then you are into very careful planning indeed - balance saddle bag, the lot. If you are based at your first night stop all the time, then life is much easier. You should always carry a first aid kit for horse and rider. You will also have to plan how to wash the girth and numnah. Remember our delightful climate and always carry a waterproof and additional warm clothing - it never pays to gamble with rain and wind.

SAFETY

It is always wiser to ride in company. The other person can always hold your horse, or pull you out of the ditch, as well as being someone to talk to about the excitements of the day and to help plan everything. You should always wear a BSI riding hat, properly secured, and also safe footwear. You need a clearly defined heel and a smooth sole. Even if riding in company, tell someone where you are going and roughly how long you expect to take. If affordable, take a portable telephone. Make a list of the things you must carry every day and check it before leaving base.

INSURANCE

You should have Third Party Legal Liability Insurance. This will protect you if you or your horse cause a bit of mayhem (accidentally!). Membership of the BHS gives you this type of insurance, plus Personal Accident Insurance as part of the membership package. Check your household insurance to make sure it covers riding before you rely only on that, as some insurances do not. You should always have this type of cover when venturing forth into the outside world, even if it is an hour's hack from home.

PARKING

If you intend to box to the start of the day's ride, either have someone to take the box away or make sure it is safely, securely and considerately parked. If you have to make arrangements to park, do it well in advance or the contact may well have gone to market or the hairdressers when you make a last minute call. Have the vehicle number etched on to the windows for security.

MONEY

This is vital, so work out a system of getting money if necessary. Sadly we can no longer gallop up to the bank and lead Dobbin into the cashier's queue, nor do most banks have hitching rails. Post Offices are more numerous and might be a useful alternative. Always have the price of a telephone call on you.

Lastly, if you do run into problems of blocked paths or boggy ones, write to the Highway Authority of the relevant county council and tell them. Then you can do something about it. You might even think of adopting a path near home and keeping an eye on it, telling your own county council of any difficulties you encounter. It is through such voluntary work that these rides have been made possible.

Wherever you ride, always do it responsibly, with care of the land, consideration for the farmer and courtesy for all other users. Remember the Country Code and enjoy your ARROW Riding.

I hope this chapter will have started you planning and making lists. If I seem to be always writing about forward planning it is only because I usually leave things to the last minute, which causes chaos!

PHILIPPA LUARD

WELCOME TO LEICESTERSHIRE & RUTLAND

Off the beaten track in Leicestershire, you will discover a wonderful variety of scenery ranging from spacious uplands to broad valleys, and much of it relatively unknown and a delight to explore.

And on horseback, you will have a vantage point to enjoy some of England's most quintessential countryside.

Charnwood Forest provides a photographer's paradise, where rock, woodland and water come together in perfect harmony. Further East, the area around Melton Mowbray provides spectacular views over the Vale of Belvoir. These two areas contain the famous Quorn, Belvoir and Cottesmore hunts.

You will need time to explore the traditional rural countryside of South Leicestershire, with its pleasant farming villages, dark spinneys and canals. North East of Market Harborough, the wide Welland Valley merges with the lonely hills of High Leicestershire where sweeping pale green pastures lead to isolated distant summits. Getting lost in a myriad of single track, gated roads is a positive pleasure.

Rutland is different again. Chocolate-box villages and quaint market towns surround the vast expanse of Rutland Water. Further South, in its truly delightful setting lies tranquil Eyebrook Reservoir, training ground in 1943 for the famous 'Dam Busters Raid'.

But Leicestershire has far more to offer than just stunning panoramas. The County is crammed full of fascinating attractions and these trails take you close to some of the best.

Relive the age of steam and follow the route of Thomas Cook's first tourism excursion from Leicester to Loughborough on the Great Central Railway.

Marvel at Snibston Discovery Park - the Middle England Visitor Attraction of the Year for 1993. Situated near Coalville, this is Leicestershire's largest and newest attraction offering a unique mix of science, nature, history and technology.

Water provides two more attractions. In the South, the Grand Union Canal climbs up to the famous Foxton Locks and down into Market Harborough while Rutland Water provides a number of activities for visitors to enjoy including Normanton Church Museum, the Butterfly and Aquatic Centre and the Nature Reserve.

Don't return home without visiting the fairytale Belvoir Castle, home of the Duke and Duchess of Rutland. The views will show you how the castle got its name.

If you're looking for entertainment, don't forget Leicestershire has fine theatres, open air Shakespeare and one of the finest programmes of festivals and culture in the country.

After all this activity, you'll want to relax, and how better than in one of the County's picturesque country pubs. You cannot leave Leicestershire without, at some stage, enjoying a 'Ploughman's Lunch' accompanied by one of the five local beers - Everards, Hoskins and Oldfield, Ruddles, Hoskins and Parish. There is even the chance to tour the Parish Brewery and sample Baz's Bonce Blower, the strongest traditionally brewed ale available on handpump in England!

If you like Stilton and Red Leicester cheeses or Pork Pies, then take the time to visit Melton Mowbray where you will find 'Ye Olde Pork Pie Shoppe', here you can see skilled bakers hand raising traditional pies, and perhaps you'll be tempted by the Original Melton Hunt Cake which is enhanced with generous amounts of Old Jamaican rum.

Here, as in many other market towns and quaint villages, you will want to browse in the arcades, the antique and craft shops and find that bargain to remind you of your stay in Leicestershire.

Take your time and you will see there is more to Leicestershire than meets the eye.

SIGNPOSTING & WAYMARKING IN EAST LEICESTERSHIRE

All bridleways are signposted at the road with green signs with a white horseshoe, unless indicated in the text.

Unclassified County Roads (UCRs) - usually shown as a 'white road' on the Ordnance Survey map - may be signposted in a variety of ways, ranging through directional sign; eg Gated/Field Road, Unsuitable for Motors, No Through Road, to nothing at all. *The text will tell you what to look for.*

Rights of Way shown as Roads Used as Public Paths (RUPPs) on the Ordnance Survey map may now have been reclassified as bridleways and signposted as such, or as Byways Open to All Traffic, where the sign may be Byway or the range indicated for Unclassified County Roads.

Prior to 1990 any waymarking done in Leicestershire used yellow arrows for all Rights of Ways so you may come across old yellow arrows on a bridleway - these will usually be wooden. The

'Waymark 2000' programme now being pursued on a parish by parish basis uses the national scheme - these will usually be metal waymarks - of blue arrows for bridleways, red for byways and yellow for footpaths. However, this started in the west of the county and is only now moving into the east where many bridleways are not yet waymarked but matters should improve during the lifetime of this book. You can expect good waymarking where the track is part of a major route such as the Mid-Shires Way for horses, or the Leicestershire Round, Viking Way, Hereward's Way and Jubilee Trail which all incorporate bridleways.

LEICESTERSHIRE AND RUTLAND ON HORSEBACK

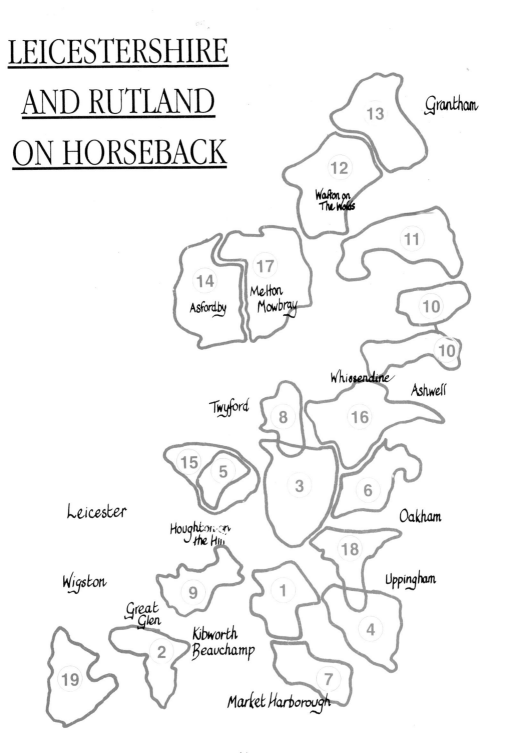

Grantham

13

12

Walton on The Wolds

11

17

14

Melton Mowbray

Asfordby

10

10

Whissendine

Ashwell

Twyford

8

16

15

5

3

6

Leicester

Oakham

Houghton on the Hill

18

Wigston

9

1

Uppingham

Great Glen

4

2

Kibworth Beauchamp

19

7

Market Harborough

THE MIDSHIRES WAY

The Midshires Way is a long-distance bridleway across Middle England, approximately 225 miles long. It links The Ridgeway with the Trans Pennine Trail and then north to reach the Pennines, thus opening up the possibility of a link with the proposed Pennine Bridleway, should this be approved.

From south to north the Midshires Way crosses Buckinghamshire, Northamptonshire, Leicestershire, Nottinghamshire, Derbyshire and the Peak National Park, before reaching the Pennines near Stockport, in Greater Manchester.

For the most part, the Midshires Way follows public bridleways or quiet country lanes.

The route will be completed in 1994, with the exception of a length in Derbyshire, from the River Trent at Long Eaton. Along this section, a footpath route has been waymarked, and a bridleway route will follow later.

Further information on each County section can be obtained as follows:

Buckinghamshire - Planning & Transportation Department - 0296 395000

Northamptonshire - Countryside Services - 0604 237220

Leicestershire - Planning & Transportation Department - 0533 657091

Nottinghamshire - Planning & Economic Development Department - 0602 774394

Derbyshire - Planning & Highways Department - 0629 580000 (Ext.7127)

Peak Park Joint Planning Board - 0629 814321

Stockport Metropolitan Borough Council - Leisure Services Department -
061 474 4420

MIDSHIRES WAY

Manchester
Stockport
Peak National Park
Buxton
Derbyshire
• Bakewell
• Matlock
Nottinghamshire
Ashbourne
Nottingham
Derby
Long Eaton
Kegworth
Loughborough
Melton Mowbray
Leicestershire
Oakham
Leicester
Uppingham
Market Harborough
Kettering
Northamptonshire
Northampton
Milton Keynes
Towcester
Bletchley
Bucks.
Buckingham
Aylesbury
Ridgeway

Midshires Way

——— Midshires Way
‑‑‑‑‑ Footpath Section
..... Trans-Pennine Trail
‑·‑·‑ Proposed Pennine Bridleway

MIDSHIRES WAY
THROUGH LEICESTERSHIRE

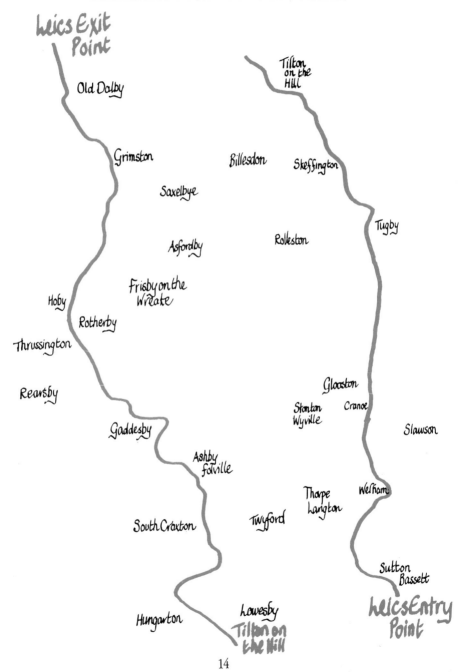

SAFETY

Know your Highway Code (1994 Edition)

In Particular Paragraphs 216/224

15

GLOOSTON

TRAIL 1

A 15 MILE CIRCULAR TRAIL (CLOCKWISE)

Ordnance Survey Maps:
Pathfinder: 895 & 916
Landranger: 141

Parking & Starting Point:
Parking is available at The Old Barn Public House in Glooston (GR.748958). Glooston is a small village situated 6 miles north of Market Harborough.

Route Description:

On leaving your parking place, head west along Andrews Lane before turning north-west along the line of the old Roman Road which ran from Leicester to Huntington. At the crossroads (GR.735962) take the track to the right. The bridleway runs northwards across five arable fields to Noseley Brook. Using the dead tree in the field over the brook as a landmark, follow the path down to the bridge which lies directly below and cross over to pass through Noseley Park to join the metalled road (GR.734990).

Turn right on to the road and continue down hill passing the road to Goadby on the right. Following the marked bridleway, turn immediately left (GR.748991). Pass through a gate and go down the steep hill to cross a brook by a bridge with handgates. *It is advisable to dismount to cross the bridge.* Follow the bridleway over two fields and through a gate onto a track which leads up the hill to Rolleston. *The lake to the left is man-made with the route passing across the dam.* **After passing**

the lake, immediately turn right taking the bridleway to Tugby (GR.735003). Go through the gateway, keeping Pops Spinney to the right and continue due east to negotiate another gate before the farm track leads to a hunting gate to cross the ford. Turn right and go through the gate and, keeping the fence to the left, follow the track to a metal gate which leads into a grass field. *There are sometimes horses in this field.* Ride up the hill to the village of Tugby. *If you require refreshments, there are two public houses here and both are open every evening and at lunchtime on Saturday and Sunday.*

At the top of the hill, turn right at the T-junction (GR.761009) and continue in a southerly direction for 1 mile until you reach another T-junction (GR.764998). Continue straight over the road and on to a small metalled track leading south to Cranoe*.

When you reach Lakes Farm, if you wish, you can take an additional loop to visit Hallaton. Hallaton Castle is here and this is one of the country's better examples of a motte and bailey. You will also find The Fox Public House, which is open each lunchtime for refreshment. See# below for instructions for this diversion.

Continue straight on up the concrete road, which becomes a grass track a little further along. Turn left through the gateway where it meets with a track coming up from the right (GR.762975). Immediately after the pond, turn right

16

TRAIL 1.

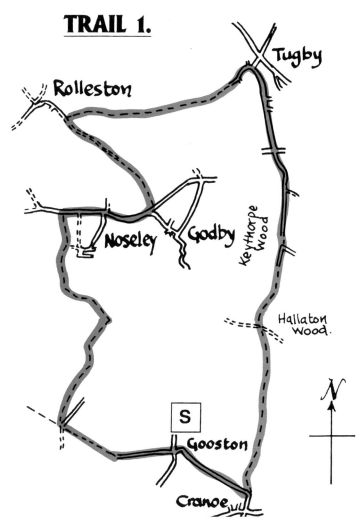

Rolleston

Tugby

Noseley

Godby

Keythorpe Wood

Hallaton Wood.

N

S

Gooston

Cranoe

Hallerton Buttercross.

onto the marked bridleway. *This track is part of The Mid-Shires Way.* **Continue due south, going through two gates, then through a third into a grass paddock to descend steeply onto a metalled road close to Cranoe Church (GR.761953). Turn right along the road and follow the road gently downhill for just under one mile to Glooston and your starting point.**

#Instructions for the diversion to Hallaton:
Turn left at the first entrance to Lakes Farm and follow the track around two large arable fields. Ride down the winding track and over a bridge. When you reach the end of the fence to your right, turn right across the field and continue up the hill, keeping the wood on your left. The track continues straight through arable fields until you come to a grass field as you near the village. Turn right after the gate and follow the hedge on your right until you come to a wooden hunting gate into a narrow lane. Turn left onto the metalled road and ride into Hallaton. You will find the The Fox Public House straight ahead at the end of the road.

To return to the original route, leave The Fox by the way you came and continue straight on the small road to the top. To see Hallaton Castle, look to your left where the road bends to the left, then right, before you ride down hill to the ford at GR.780969. Cross the ford and in approximately one mile take the bridleway to the left which runs alongside a hedge in a large arable field. Be sure and turn on to the bridleway before the hedge starts and not go through the gate into a grass field. You have now rejoined the main route (GR.762975).

The Old Grammar School.

18

FOXTON LOCKS

TRAIL 2

A 19 MILES CIRCULAR TRAIL (CLOCKWISE)

Ordnance Survey Maps:
Pathfinder: 916 & 937
Landranger: 140 &141

Parking & Starting Point:
Limited parking is available at Foxton Locks (GR.693898)only by prior arrangement with Mrs Matts (telephone 0533 792657) who will tell you exactly where to p a r k. Alternative parking can be found in North Lane at the north end of Foxton village.

Route Description:

Cross the bridge taking you over the Grand Union Canal and locks and follow the waymarked bridleway across grass fields to a metalled road (GR.686896). Turn right up the hill to Gumley and soon after passing The Bell Public House turn left through a gate into a field,onto the marked bridleway. *This bridleway is a narrow track.* Ride straight ahead across the field to the next gate. Go through the gate and follow the waymarks into another field, down a steep hill, keeping the big trees on the right, to the headland and then ride towards the wooden farm gate going through and into a grass paddock.

Cross the paddock to a small gate at a bridge. Cross over the bridge and then swing slightly left across the corner of the field to a metal gate. Cross the next field diagonally on a track to the

headland by a tall hedge and ride into the next arable field. Continue up the hill passing to the left of a clump of trees to a small gate in the hedge.

Cross the field to a holding pen through hunting gates. Ride through the next field, pass through a metal gate and ride diagonally across the next field to a wooden safety pen and go through the hunting gate onto a metalled road (GR.668883).

Turn right at Laughton road and ride around the village until reaching an Unclassified County Road at GR.661891. *This is a stony track.* Cross two small grass fields diagonally to the left. Ride over two further fields and through a metal gate onto a concrete bridge. *It may be necessary to dismount to open this gate.* Pick up a gravel track to join the Mowsley road (GR.655904). Turn right towards Saddington, passing Jacqui's Tea Rooms on the right and continue through Saddington village passing the Queens Head Public House on the right.

Having passed the Public House take the left hand fork north of the village (GR.656922) to Fleckney then take the bridleway to the left at GR.653927 to meet the Arnesby road. Ride straight over following the road west towards Arnesby for 0.75 miles. Immediately after passing Grange Farm take the first bridleway right (GR.628923) to

19

Fleckney. Turn left on the metalled road to the village. Turn right at the T-junction in the village (GR.649934), then first left into Kibworth Road. Turn left at the second Kibworth road sign into a cul-de-sac with cottages on both sides. Go through the gate at the end on the bridleway eastwards to Smeeton Westerby. Cross the Grand Union Canal by going over a concrete bridge and ride over the Kibworth road into Mill Lane (GR.663933). *There is good visibility at the road crossing. In the lane there are good views to the north of Billesdon Coplow and to the south of Gumley Park*

Follow the lane down into Smeeton Westerby to meet the village street at a T-junction. *Stop and listen for vehicles. Traffic is not very heavy, but there is poor visibility.* Turn right past the Kings Head Public House on the right and after a further 70 yards take the first left into Debdale Lane (GR.679928). Follow the track to Debdale Wharf to the metalled lane (GR.695916). Turn right and follow the lane to the end, where you meet the road to Gumley. Here you continue straight on up the hill to follow the road around to the left and down the hill into Gumley village. Pass The Bell Public House on the left and retrace your tracks along the bridleway to the metalled road at GR.686896 and retrace your steps to Foxton Locks Car Park and your starting point.

TRAIL 2

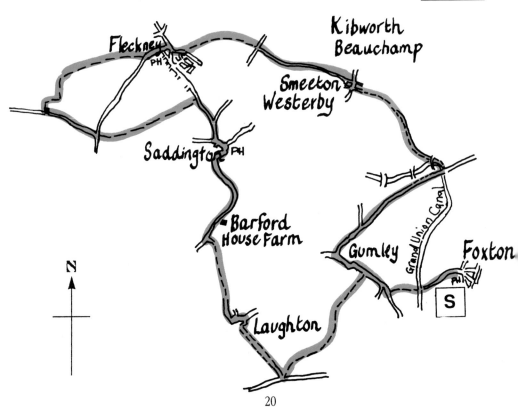

LAUNDE TO TILTON

TRAIL 3

A 15 MILE CIRCULAR TRAIL (ANTI-CLOCKWISE)

Ordnance Survey Maps:
Pathfinder: 895 & 896
Landranger: 141

Parking & Starting Point:
Parking is available south-west of Tilton on the Hill on the 'Back Road' to Loddington between the B6047 and Tilton on the Hill (GR.739053), approximately 1.50 miles north of its intersection with the A47 (GR.740057). It is also available at Launde Abbey (GR.795044) by prior arrangement with the Warden. Please telephone Belton 254.

Route Description:

Ride along the Loddington road out of Tilton on the Hill and turn right going through a wooden gate onto the marked bridleway, just before, and opposite, the last house (GR.744052). *You are now on the Mid-shires Way.* Follow the stone track through the first two fields and go through a wooden gate alongside the cattle grid. Continue on to pass through a small paddock with a barn conversion to your left and ride on through three gates to the Eye Brook. Cross over a small bridge and into an enormous arable field. Follow the track, keeping roughly parallel to the hedge on the left until you come to a bridge where you can cross the deep ditch. Ride in the same south-south easterly direction and aim for an iron gate with a sign. Cross the stone track and go through a signed gate into a grass field. Cross this field, diagonally to the

left to another iron gate. Go through the gate and into an arable field. Follow the hedge-line down hill and before the stream, go through the gate in the hedge on the left and turn right to immediately descend into the trees and cross the brook by an old brick bridge which is hidden under the trees. *As the trees are low and you are entering a darker area, a rider may choose to dismount before crossing the bridge.*

Follow the track up the hill to a gate and continue along the track until you meet the A47 (GR.755019). Turn left and with great care, ride along the road for a few yards until you meet the bridleway on the left. Turn here heading due east across a field to a gap in the corner where you pick up the farm track which leads to the road (GR.766017). Turn right along the road and then go left onto the bridleway which is just before the trees. Follow this track past the farm buildings on the left. *Take in the lovely views of high Leicestershire to the north-east.* Go through the hunting gate into a large arable field and keep the hedge to your right until it ends, when you strike off diagonally to your left aiming for the brick buildings at the other side of the stream.

The ford is waymarked, but if the corn is high it is not always possible to see it, however there is a telegraph pole nearby which makes a good landmark. You will find a lovely old paved ford which is not deep. Cross the ford and follow the track up through the brick buildings and go through an iron gate into the woods. Go through the woods and as you leave them, look immediately to your left to see the very small and charming Loddington Church.

Continue along the track going through a very long ford to eventually meet the Loddington road (GR.788020). Here, ride straight on up the hill and turn right at the T-junction (GR.789024) Follow the road round to the left and up a long hill to pass through a gate which is situated next to a cattle grid and so into Launde Park. Ride along the gated road which takes you down the steep hill to find Launde Abbey Retreat Centre at the bottom on your right. *Parking is available here.* Proceed through the gate at the side of the cattle grid and go straight ahead to follow the gated road past the fishing ponds over the River Chater, up and down hill until you meet the main road (GR.804062). Taking care, cross over the road onto the marked bridleway. After 200 yards, go left through a gap in the hedge and ride diagonally across the field to a metal gate. Go through the gate, cross three grass fields and then branch north onto the unmarked bridleway to Knossington (GR.807067).

After crossing the River Gwash ascend the grass field and aim for the wooden gate to the left of Windmill Lodge and garden and so into the grass lane to meet the Braunston road (GR.804083) where you turn left into the village of Knossington. Almost immediately you turn left onto the Owston road, crossing over the first cross roads and continuing on until you reach the Somerby road. Here you can EITHER go straight over and into the lane to

turn left at the T-junction, right at Oundle Farm and so miss the village, OR, you can turn left at the first T-junction and then take the second turning on the right and so into the charming, little village, to follow the village street round to turn left at Oundle Farm.

Proceed down Washdyke road a little until you meet the marked bridleway to the right (GR.771080). Go through the metal gate, *where you may have to dismount,* and follow the track through the fields to Owston Lodge Farm and ride on into the farm yard. *You may have to pause for a moment in the farm yard if the farmer is working, but if you are fortunate he will open the gates for you and help you on your journey.* Proceed through the yard and down the farm drive meeting Dawson's Lane. Turn right to White House Farmhouse and then go left just before the house and so around to the back of their stables to continue along the bridle track. *You may have to unhook a strand of wire here in order to continue.*

Ride along the track keeping the Lodge on your right, then cross the hedge-line by way of a farm gate to go into a field. Keep left, going through the electric fence via the hooked opening if necessary. *You may have to dismount to do this.* Follow the track along the side of the wire until you come to an iron gate leading into a huge arable field. Go into the field and straight across, to continue across two more arable fields, taking care when crossing as there is a blind ditch. To find the bridge and avoid falling into the blind ditch, count from the brook to your right to the fourth tree, where it meets a lump of hedge coming from the left. Aim for the left-hand, south, end of the viaduct and pass underneath going through a

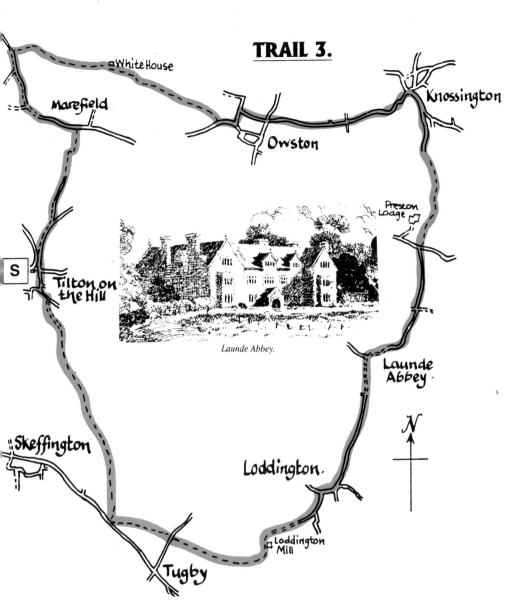

TRAIL 3.

White House

Marefield

Knossington

Owston

Preston Lodge

Launde Abbey.

S

Tilton on the Hill

Launde Abbey .

Skeffington

Loddington.

N

Loddington Mill

Tugby

wooden gate into a grass field. Go straight along the track to a gated road. Turn left (GR.739090), then bear left under the disused railway bridge (GR.741081) to Marefield.

Go through the hamlet and take the Unclassified County Road to your right (GR.749079). *This is waymarked with a* .horseshoe and footprint. **Ride through the old iron gate,** *again you may need to dismount,* **and onto a stony track. This pretty track will take you along through various wobbly gates and shallow fords, climbing steeply giving you super views of Burrough Hill, Melton Mowbray and beyond, to arrive at Tilton on the Hill and your starting point.**

TRAIL 4

A 17 MILE CIRCULAR TRAIL (CLOCKWISE)

Ordnance Survey Maps:
Pathfinder: 916 & 917
Landranger: 141

Parking & Starting Point:
Park on the good roadside verge just north of Great Easton, on the Stockerston road (GR.846934). Great Easton is approximately 1.25 miles west of Caldecott on the A6003 between Uppingham and Corby.

Route Description:

Leaving the parking point ride back towards the village and take the first turn right down Broadgate. Bear right at the end of this road and ride on until you come to a wooden gate. Pass through the gate and follow the track onto the signed bridleway round to the left and close to bushes. Go through a waymarked bridlegate into a narrow corridor and out through another bridlegate. Turn right and follow a brook through three grass fields and then four arable fields.

Ride through two further wooden gates and then diagonally across to the far right corner of a grass field into an arable field, then left riding towards a small metal gate straight ahead. Ride along with the fence on your left through a farm gate and continue half way along the fence until you meet a bridlegate across a stream on the path. Go through this gate and head north-west to rejoin the bridleway on the far side of a triangle

of trees. Bear left and head for a metal gate which is adjacent to the Drayton road (GR.816934). *The triangle of trees houses a gun club. They shoot once a fortnight at 10.00 am on Sundays from Sept-April inc. and every other Monday from 7.00 pm onwards from May - Aug inc. If your horse is not used to gun fire then avoid these days and times.*

At the road turn right and ride on to pass the school 100 metres after a road to the left, take the bridleway on the left (GR.815937) through a grass field and on down to cross the B664 Uppingham road (GR.808943) which is not busy. Follow the waymarked bridleway up the other side and go diagonally left across an arable field aiming for a single tree on the horizon. Ride over the top and down the other side where you meet the Blaston track (GR.800950). Here turn right and then soon afterwards turn left onto a short, signposted bridleway which brings you to the Hallaton road (GR.801955). Turn left and then right at the T-junction (GR.793953). Ride on into the village of Hallaton. In the village turn right at the T-junction to the Fox Inn. Take the road towards East Norton, then turn right again (GR.790972) on Allexton road. After 1.25 miles turn right through wooden gates on to an Unclassified County Road, *(this is not marked on the Ordnance Survey map),* (GR.803983) opposite the turning to Fearn Farm and ride straight across a grass field onto the track to Horninghold.

In Horninghold, turn left at the T-junction and ride through the village, pass a turning on your right and then take a bridleway on your right (GR.813974) immediately after passing Horninghold Wood. At the top corner of an arable field, cross into a grass field through a small bridlegate on your right. Bear left downhill, with the hedge on your left. Ride straight on between the woods in a narrowing field and through a wooden gate at the end. Pick up the grass track on the other side and follow it all the way to Stockerston. *The Hall which you pass on the left is the home of the de Lisles.* After passing the Hall leave the field through a very narrow wooden gate on your left. Turn right onto a small metalled lane and ride downhill to a T-junction with a B road (GR.838976). **TAKE GREAT CARE, TRAFFIC CAN BE HEAVY AND FAST HERE.** Turn right and ride for 100 yards on this busy road to a bend where you continue straight on into a pretty lane to the Eyebrook Reservoir.

Passing the Eyebrook Reservoir keep straight ahead at the junction and follow the reservoir round on the metalled road, with good verges, until the road meets the Great Easton road (GR.843941). Here turn left and go gently downhill to your starting point.

Eyebrook Reservoir belongs to Stuart & Lloyds and supplied the steel industry at Corby. It is now used only when needed and for emergencies. It is a prominent wild fowl sanctuary and if you have binoculars, you will see all manner of species.

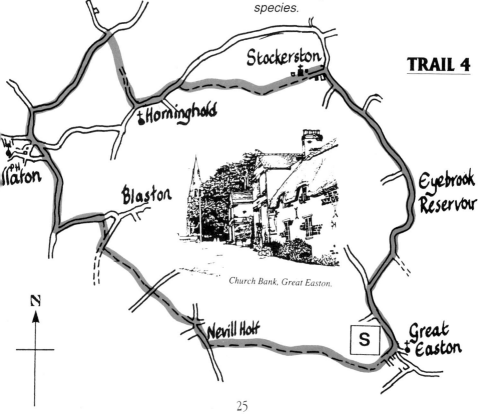

TRAIL 4

Church Bank, Great Easton.

N

A 13 MILE CIRCULAR TRAIL (CLOCKWISE)

Ordnance Survey Maps:
Landranger: 140 & 141
Pathfinder: 895

Parking & Starting Point:
Parking is available on the good wide verges in Enderby Lane (GR.719056) between Sludge Hall Farm and Cold Newton. Your starting point is at Cold Newton 1.75 miles north-west of Tilton-on-the-Hill.

Route Description:

Ride north-west along Enderby's Lane towards Cold Newton. Pass the right turn to the village and take the bridleway (GR.713064) on the left to Quenby Hall. *This is the seat of Squire DeLisle.* A little way after passing Quenby Hall you will see a bridlegate on your left alongside a wire fence (GR.698063). Go through this gate and follow the bridleway south-west and across three large arable fields to come to a ford at the bottom of the last field. Cross the ford and go through the farm gate onto a road (GR.689058).

Turn right along the road, then go immediately left to Old Ingarsby. At the top of the hill and on the right-hand bend outside Ingarsby Old Hall, turn left onto a bridleway and skirt the site of a medieval village. After passing an old and broken fence line, turn right down the hill to come to a farm gate just to the right of the stream. Go through

the gate and onto a road where you turn left, then immediately right to go through a gate and up the track, passing Monk's Grave on your right. Continue on, going through a gate into the next field and then through another gate at the north-west corner of the field into a wide, grass lane. Ride along the lane, then before the lane narrows, go right through a gate and into a grass field. Continue northwards through fields and over an old railway bridge.

Ride on down a farm track and, where the track bends right, do not follow to the bottom, but turn left. Follow the hedge line on your right and before you reach the brook, turn right through a cattle pen and into a field. Follow the line of the brook on your left and go over the farm bridge and into the lane for Keyham, going through The Kennels. *There is a nice Public House on the right in the village - The Dog & Gun - and it is open at lunch times should you wish to take a break.*

At the T-junction in Keyham (GR.670067), turn right, then take the first left and after a short distance, take the bridleway to your left (GR.673067), which runs north to Hungarton Lane. On meeting the lane (GR.679076), turn right and pass two right turns, crossing into Baggrave Park at South Lodge. *To see Baggrave Hall, follow the estate road round to the left then go right to pass the medieval site of the village and continue to ride on as far as Queniborough Brook for a view of the house.* **Retrace your steps and after the road bends left, you keep straight on going through a bridlegate (GR.696082).** Continue along the bridleway going south-east to meet a bridleway coming in from the left (GR.720069) and so ride on in a south-easterly direction across a field to **Inkerman Lodge.** *There are often horses in the small grass field immediately before the farm so do be considerate. The gates are easy to open and close but the gate at the bottom of the field has a bushy corridor leading up to it which must be empty of livestock before you go in to open the gate.*

On leaving the field, cross straight over the drive through an iron gate and then across a field, keeping the fence on your left, to come to a bridlegate leading into a dark wood. Go through the gate and into the wood. *As the track here is narrow, it is easier to dismount to open and shut the gate, so leading your horse into the wood.* **Go through the wood and cross over the road on the other side with White's Barn to your right by a cattle grid. Ride parallel to the hedge following the blue arrow waymarkings across two fields then, with the hedge on the right, meet and cross the brook to come to a small bridlegate. Bear left across the next field to come to a road (GR.719068).**

Turn right on this road and when the road bends right into a farm yard, carry straight on through a gate and follow the fence on your right. *On the other side of the fence you can clearly see the site of a medieval village.* **At the end of this track you will meet Enderby Lane. Turn left along the lane to return to your parking place.**

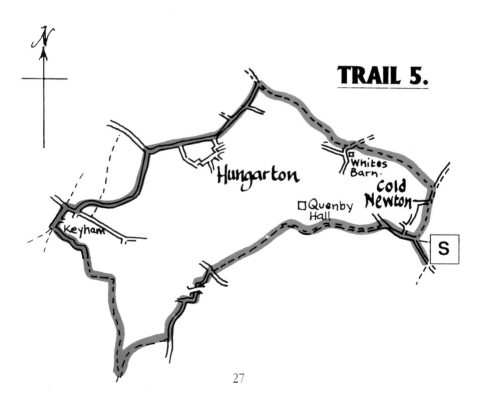

TRAIL 5.

27

LAUNDE TO BRAUNSTON

TRAIL 6

A 11 MILE CIRCULAR TRAIL (ANTI-CLOCKWISE)

Ordnance Survey Maps:
Pathfinder: 895 & 896
Landranger: 141

Parking & Starting Point:
Parking is available at Launde Abbey by prior arrangement with the Warden, (telephone Belton 254) (GR.795044).

Route Description:

Leave your parking place at Launde Abbey by the gate alongside the cattle grid, on the road which winds north-east over the River Chater, passing the fishing ponds to meet the Oakham road (GR.804062). Cross over the road and go on to the marked bridleway. After 200 yards, go left through a gap in the hedge and ride diagonally across the next field to the metal gate. Go through the gate and cross three grass fields taking care not to divert onto the bridleway which heads north for Knossington at GR.807067.

Follow the grass track and with the hedge on your right, go through a gap in the hedge and bear slightly right to continue down the track with the hedge now on your left. Turn left with the grass track when you reach the bottom of the field and the hedge is now on your right. At the end of this field continue on the bridleway (GR.813069). Ride through a small hunting gate and cross a small field bearing slightly left, to go through a metal gate in the corner to enter the next field which you also

go straight across, keeping the right hand hedgerow 100 yards to your right and so follow on down to a metal gate and ford. *Either side of the ford, the ground is soft, but the ford itself is good and not deep.* Cross the ford and follow the lane until you come to the road (GR.818074) and cross straight over and onto another marked bridleway.

Ride diagonally across the first field and go through a hunting gate into the next field which you also cross, again to a hunting gate, which you go through and ride along a track between two overgrown hedges to meet the junction with the marked bridleway to Braunston (GR.826079). Turn right onto this bridleway heading for Braunston-in-Rutland. Follow this bridleway across two fields, to turn right through a farm gate just before the end of the second field. This takes you into a lane which will lead you down to Braunston village. *Here you will find the excellent Blue Bell Public House at the south end of the village.*

Leave Braunston on the Oakham road. *This is quite a busy road but there is good visibility.* At the top of the hill turn right opposite Hill Top Farm onto the marked bridleway (GR.843078). Turn right, heading south-east, crossing a small metalled road (GR.852071) and continue through two more fields to meet a marked bridleway coming from the left (GR.855068). Turn right and

28

follow this track over to Bridge Farm and then on to Brooke. When you meet the metalled road, go straight ahead, following the road round past Brooke Priory to your right, turning left shortly after towards Braunston (GR.846063).

Take the next turn left onto the marked bridleway (GR.842065) to take you by the pumping station. *This is a very pretty route which starts in a grass field and becomes a grass track that passes by grass fields where horses graze.* When you reach the metalled road (GR.836056), turn left, then at Hibbitts Lodge turn right (GR.839054) and ride down the paved farm road to Leigh Lodge. When you reach the farm yard, turn right (GR.828041) and follow the track which runs parallel to, and just to the north of the River Chater. Pass the marked bridleway coming on to the track from the left at GR.814044. When you come to some rough ground and trees, bear left going closer to the river to pick up a small path which takes you over into a large grass field. Ride diagonally across this field and go through the gate at the top corner and into the next field. Cross this field to leave through a gate at the back of Launde Abbey to join the road from Launde, just north of the gate and cattle grid and your starting point.

TRAIL 6.

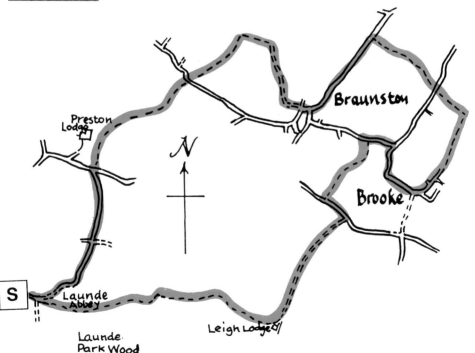

STONTON WYVILLE

TRAIL 7

A 12 MILE CIRCULAR TRAIL (CLOCKWISE)

Ordnance Survey Maps:
Pathfinder: 916 & 917
Landranger: 141

Parking & Starting Point:
Parking is available in the lane to the south of the Cranoe/Harborough road (GR.738946). There is a good verge here and no traffic in the lane.

Route Description:

Leave your parking place and take the lane north to Stonton Wyville. Cross the Cranoe road and turn right in Stonton Wyville to ride north along the hard road which eventually degenerates into a gravel track. When you reach the gate, pass through into the grass field and follow the track north across the field to meet the Roman Road at GR.735962.

Turn right towards Glooston and follow the road into the village. There is an excellent public house on your right 'The Old Barn'. Ride straight over the crossroads and bear right to Cranoe. Go down the steep hill into the village and cross the main road (GR.761950) to go south onto Welham Lane.

Continue along the lane to take the bridleway on the left (GR.760946) and so onto The Mid-Shires Way. Follow the brook on the right hand side to ride south-east across several fields crossing Welham Road and then Green Lane until you meet Ashley Road at GR 795928. *Some gates along this bridlepath will require you to dismount and you may possibly encounter an electric fence just before you meet the main road.*

Turn right onto the main road (GR.795928). *Take care here, there is sometimes heavy traffic, but you have excellent visibility in both directions.* **Cross over the Welland River and pass Ashley Station which is now disused and when you reach a right-hand bend leading to Ashley village, turn left through the gate to take the bridleway west at GR.793909.**

Keeping the hedge to your left, follow the bridleway for one field and then go through two more fields with the hedge on your right. When you come to the gate, go through and onto the track which runs south across an arable field to Five Ways (GR.782899), where five bridleways meet. Take the bridleway west towards Sutton Bassett, going immediately through a gate and down the hill across two grass fields. *You are requested not to gallop down here by the farmer at Lodge Farm.* Ride through the farm yard and into the lane and on to meet the main Market Harborough road (GR.770898). Cross straight over the main road and go towards Market Harborough to take the bridleway which is almost immediately to your right at GR.769898. Follow this north-west across grass meadows, crossing the Welland River on a narrow wooden

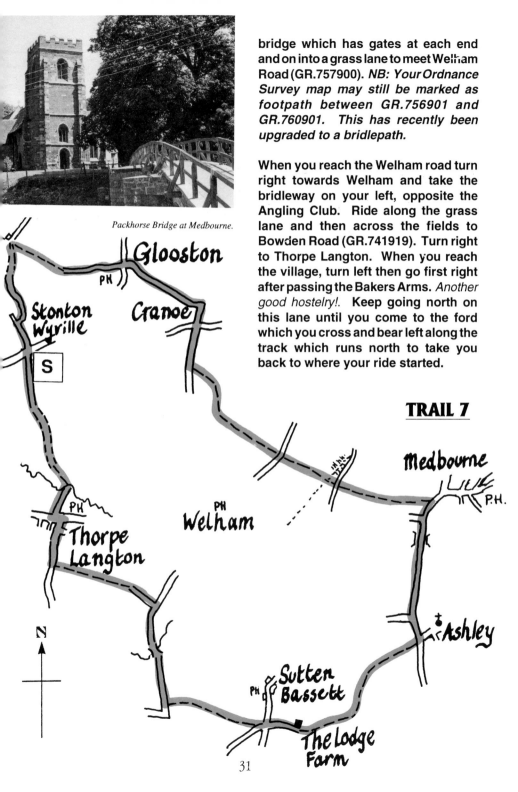

bridge which has gates at each end and on into a grass lane to meet Welham Road (GR.757900). *NB: Your Ordnance Survey map may still be marked as footpath between GR.756901 and GR.760901. This has recently been upgraded to a bridlepath.*

When you reach the Welham road turn right towards Welham and take the bridleway on your left, opposite the Angling Club. Ride along the grass lane and then across the fields to Bowden Road (GR.741919). Turn right to Thorpe Langton. When you reach the village, turn left then go first right after passing the Bakers Arms. *Another good hostelry!.* Keep going north on this lane until you come to the ford which you cross and bear left along the track which runs north to take you back to where your ride started.

Packhorse Bridge at Medbourne.

TRAIL 7

Glooston

Stonton Wyrille

Cranoe

S

Medbourne

P.H.

Welham

Thorpe Langton

N

Ashley

Sutton Bassett

The Lodge Farm

BURROUGH HILL

TRAIL 8

A 10 MILE CIRCULAR TRAIL (CLOCKWISE)

Ordnance Survey Maps:
Pathfinder: 875 & 895
Landranger: 129 & 141

Parking & Starting Point:
Park on the good grass verges which are to be found in Washdyke Road, between the small villages of Owston and Marefield (GR.759077) which can be reached via the B6047 Melton to Tilton road from the west and via the Tilton to Oakham road from the south. This is also your starting point.

Of Interest:
This ride follows only quiet roads and bridleways. It is very hilly in parts and the going is good. There is a shallow ford to cross at Newbold and Burrough Hill's Iron Age Fort is a place of interest.

Route Description:

Riding from your parking point (GR.759077) take the Unclassified County Road going due north-east from this point. This is a track running up the west side of arable fields with a hedge on the left and goes to Newbold. At the bottom of the hill, cross the ford; then climb up the stone track to a T-junction in Newbold (GR.765091). At the T-junction turn left onto the metalled lane and follow this up and down a hill, crossing a bridleway at GR.760093. *At this crossing pause a moment and look ahead and to the left across the valley at the little hedged grass lane which runs east-west; this is the track you will be*

following. **Continue straight along the lane to the bottom of the hill, where you cross the brook and go through the gateway to turn immediately left across a field to the gate opposite. Go through the gate and into a hedged grass lane. Continue up the hill and through a gate into a large grass field and leaving the water trough on the right, bear left down to the gate onto a metalled road (GR.753094).**

At this road, turn right and go up the hill to meet the Twyford-Burrough road where you turn right again and after 600 yards turn left down Melton Lane, which is signposted to Great Dalby. Follow this road down the hill. *As the hedge to your right becomes lower you will be able to see an impressive view of Burrough Hill Monument.*

After approximately one mile this road is crossed by an Unclassified County Road which is signposted to Burrough Hill. Turn right (GR.752119) onto this grass track and go through the wooden gate at the top into the monument field. Be careful to follow the track here as horses are not allowed on the ramparts. *Looking to your right you will see Burrough Village with Billesdon Coplow beyond.* **When you come to the big thorn tree take the small stoned track to go straight ahead between the gorse bushes and through the gulley to come to a wooden gate. Go through the gate to the notice board for the Country Park (GR.763117).** *It is suggested you*

32

read the notice board before you ride on as you have a choice of routes here.

EITHER:

i)   The most pleasurable alternative is the Dalby Hills Path which is a permissive route and as such is not always available. This information is given below the notice board. Although the path is not marked on a Pathfinder map, it can be found on some Landranger maps as a black dashed line. If you follow the waymarked path you will come to the road between Little Dalby and Pickwell, opposite the farm entrance to Debdale Lodge (GR.781127) where you turn right for Pickwell Village.

OR

ii)   The alternative route is to ride along the bridleway running due north from the monument towards Little Dalby. You continue past the notice board and go slightly down hill on the track and follow the waymarked bridleway to go left through the wooden gate and into a grass field to continue through the next gateway to the left of the farm. Ride straight ahead across fields until you meet the metalled road (GR.766128). Turn right onto the road to join the Pickwell Road which comes in from the left and follow this to Pickwell Village.

From either of the above routes continue as follows:
Ride straight through Pickwell and on to Somerby. Turn right (GR.782105) into the High Street. Pass the Post Office and newsagents on the left, then the Old Brewery Inn and then directly opposite the Old Forge, turn left into Manor Lane. Take the signposted bridleway at the end of the lane and go through the gate into a field. Follow the line of the telegraph poles down the valley and keeping them, and the brook

to the left, ride through three fields. You can now see Owston village which lies straight ahead of you.

When the line of telegraph poles ends, continue on down the hill keeping the brook to the left and go through two metal gates. At the bottom of the hill, go into an arable field. Still with the brook to the left, ride on to come to a wooden bridge, (GR.775094) which you cross to turn right. Follow the rough grass verge and continue along the waymarked bridleway to the metal gates leading into Newbold Lane (GR.775084). Go through the metal gates and onto the lane, turning right at Oundle Farm, continue straight ahead towards Owston and proceed along Washdyke Road to your starting point.

TRAIL 8

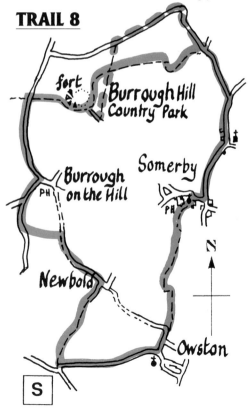

33

EIGHT VILLAGES

TRAIL 9

A 15 MILE CIRCULAR TRAIL (ANTI-CLOCKWISE)

Ordnance Survey Maps:
Pathfinder: 895 & 916
Landranger: 141

Parking & Starting Point:
At the lay-by on the B6047 just south of New Inn and the entrance to Rolleston Park (GR.723996).

Parking Note: If you park in the layby on the B6047 there is approximately 200 yards of fast road before you reach the start at Rolleston Gates. It may also be possible to park in Rolleston village, by the sign post.

Route Note: The bridleway from Billesdon to Ashlands gets ploughed in the autumn and the wood at Ashlands is very muddy then too, so it would be best to go by road to Gaulby at this time of year. Another way of avoiding the plough and shortening the ride would be to leave out Billesdon and ride across to Ashlands via Cranhill Farm from Rolleston.

Route Description:

Turn right out of the lay-by onto the main road and ride for 250 yards to turn right into Rolleston Lodge gates at New Inn. Follow the left forking track along Chestnut Avenue until reaching a metalled road in the village (GR.723999). Carry on along this road turning left into Bushby Road (GR.731004) at Rolleston and follow this track north-west until reaching the B6047 (GR.723016). Turn right and travel for 200 yards heading left into a small road leading to Billesdon. *There*

is a good verge on this busy B road. **Ride along this road to the outskirts of Billesdon and take the first left at GR.721024.** *Billesdon is an interesting village and riders may wish to detour here.*

Ride along the Gaulby road passing the school and then take a signed bridleway on the left. Ride straight ahead across a meadow to a gate at the bottom, then south diagonally across the next meadow, through a bridlegate in the corner and then follow the track over arable fields crossing a byway to Ashlands road (GR.715004). Do not come out onto the road but take the bridlegate 50 yards to the right, in a hedge facing you. Go diagonally across this meadow following the back wall of Ashlands Garden and then down to a gate in the corner of the wood. *It can be very muddy here in wet weather.* **Turn right on emerging from the wood and follow the hedge through several meadows to a road 0.50 miles south of Gaulby (GR.700005).**

Ride on towards Gaulby and at the outskirts of the village take the right-hand fork past the church where you turn left and then straight ahead down a narrow lane to Kings Norton where there is another fine church (GR.689004). Turn right up the hill through the village and then left at the T-junction. After about 50 yards take the signed bridleway on your right. This track crosses two arable fields, goes to the right of the wood and is

TRAIL 9.

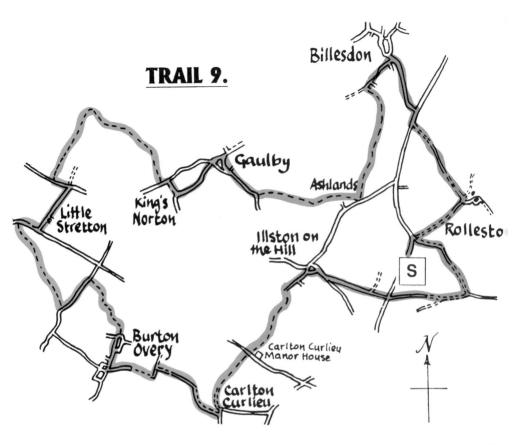

Carlton Curlieu Hall, Palmer.

then easily followed down to the stream and up to the next wood, then gently down to the River Sence (GR.676018). Turn left after crossing the river. The bridleway is not easy to see here, but continue beside the stream through the bridlegate and then on a good track across several fields until you come to a metalled road. (GR.669007).

Turn left here and then after a short distance take the first right and ride through on this minor road to Little Stretton. Pass through the village and at the top of the hill turn right and follow this road for 0.25 miles. A well marked bridleway on the left (GR.663001), opposite the next junction, will lead you back across fields in a south-easterly direction to Burton Overy. Turn left when you reach the road (GR.671988) to go north-east for 0.33 miles where you take the bridleway on the right across fields which bring you to the northern end of Burton Overy (GR.679984). Ride straight down through the village to The Bell Public House. Turn left here and up the hill towards Carlton Curlieu. Go right at the second cattle grid out of Burton Overy and on into Carlton Curlieu. *The churchyard here is full of snowdrops and aconites early in the year.* At the T-junction turn left (GR.694972). *The Hall is worth a few moments detour to the right.* After a few hundred yards a bridleway starts between hedges and leads to Carlton Curlieu Manor on the Gartree road (GR.698981). Cross straight over and follow the track through a little yard, then meadows and a field to Illston-on-the-Hill (GR.704991).

Turn right in the village (GR.707993) passing the Village Hall and right at the T-junction. Then take the left fork down to the B6047. CARE THIS IS A BUSY ROAD. Cross straight over and go up the hill bearing left at the next junction (GR.727990), then turn left to take a high, narrow, open road with magnificent views in all directions. This brings you to the back gate of Rolleston Park and the Lodge Gates and your starting point, are straight ahead. Turn left on B6047 and proceed along the grass verge 250 yards to the lay-by where you parked.

The Old School House, 1650 - Billesdon

CODE FOR RIDING & DRIVING RESPONSIBLY

THE BRITISH
HORSE SOCIETY

1. **Riders and carriage drivers** everywhere should proceed with courtesy, care and consideration. The British Horse Society recommends the following:

Care for the Land

Do not stray off the line of the path;

Do not damage timber or hedgerows by jumping;

Remember that horses' hooves can damage surfaces in bad weather;

Pay particular attention to protected areas that have significant historical and/or biological value, as they are extremely sensitive to damage.

Courtesy to other users

Remember that walkers, cyclists and other riders may be elderly, disabled, children or simply frightened of horses; whenever possible acknowledge courtesy shown by drivers of motor vehicles.

Consideration for the farmer

Shut the gate behind you;

Ride slowly past all stock;

Do not ride on cultivated land unless the right of way crosses it;

Dogs are seldom welcome on farmland or moorland unless on a lead or under close control.

2. **Observe local byelaws**

3. **Ride or drive with care on the roads** and take the BHS Riding and Road Safety Test. Always make sure that you can be seen at night or in bad visibility, by wearing the right kind of reflective/fluorescent aids.

4. **Groups from riding establishments** should contain reasonable numbers, for reasons of both safety and amenity. They should never exceed twenty in total **including** the relevant number of escorts as indicated in BHS guidelines on levels of capability among riders in groups, available on request. Rides should not deviate from the right of way or permitted route and regard must be shown at all times for growing crops, shutting and securing of gates and the consideration and courtesy due to others.

5. **Always obey the Country Code in every way possible:**

Enjoy the countryside and respect its life and work

Guard against all risk of fire

Fasten all gates

Keep your dogs under close control

Keep to public paths across farmland

Use gates and stiles to cross fences, hedges and walls

Leave livestock, crops and machinery alone

Take your litter home

Help keep all water clean

Protect wildlife, plants and trees

Take special care on country roads

Make no unnecessary noise.

GARTHORPE

TRAIL 10

A 22 MILE TRAIL
(ANTI-CLOCKWISE)

Ordnance Survey Maps:
Pathfinder: 855 & 876
Landranger: 130

Parking & Starting Points:
Parking is available at the south end of Garthorpe on the Wymondham road just off the B676 (GR.833208). Garthorpe is situated on the B676, 6.50 miles northeast of Melton Mowbray.

Route Note: A quick glance at the map shows that there are several alternatives to that described thus offering shorter routes to suit the individual rider.

Route Description:

Proceed, riding south along the road for 1.75 miles to Wymondham. In the village turn left onto the main road and then right into Nurses Lane. Follow the lane round to the left and then across the next road into Wrights Lane. From here go straight onto the bridleway (GR.857187). Cross the brook and bear right staying on the bridleway, through the gate and along the edge of the field. Go through the handgate and along the path through the woods. Continue along the narrow track with the wall on your right.

When you meet the road, turn left (GR.860177) and take the next track on the right going towards Hall Farm. Ride along this track for a few hundred yards. Before you reach the hill, turn right go through the handgate and ride onto a bridleway going across a field. Remain at the bottom of the hill and follow the bridleway by some trees to another handgate. Go through, turn left and then follow this bridleway along the hedge to some woods. Ride straight through the wood, and after crossing a bridge turn immediately right. Follow this track around the wood turning right at the bottom end and continue riding straight on along the track to a gate at the bottom of the hill. Go through the gate and straight on with water to your right. Bear right across a field and through a gate into a lane.

Cross over the road and ride straight on through a gate and into Catmose Lodge farmyard. Ride straight ahead between cattle pens and the hedge. Follow the bridleway alongside the hedge around the edge of the field to a handgate. DO NOT RIDE DIAGONALLY ACROSS THE FIELD. Turn right onto a road and follow the road over the railway crossing to the T-junction (GR.825171). Turn left and go over the bridge to take the next left turning up the drive to Holygate Farm (GR.821170). Take the right-hand fork into the farmyard and follow the concrete drive round to the new barn. Pass to the right of the barn and then turn right on to a track. Keeping the hedge on the left, follow the track to, and along the top of the hill and then go left through a gap in the hedge which is beside a large tree. Ride down the hill, through the gate and keep straight on to the next gate. Follow the hedge for a few yards to the next gate on the right, go through the gate and follow the track straight across the field to a gate in the middle of the hedge. Go through the gate and straight across this field, through another gate and alongside the hedge on the left to come to a gateway by the farmyard. Turn left onto a metalled road (GR.825147) and follow the road to Whissendine. At the junction in the village turn left, down hill and over the bridge, then go up the hill towards the church. Just beyond the church, turn left (GR.834142). After 200 yards turn right onto a track (GR.834146). Follow this track down to some houses and then, WITH CARE, across a railway line. Ride on to the end of the track to meet a road. Turn left along the road and take the first right turn to Market Overton.

Ride along the Market Overton road until you come to the point where it bends sharply to the left (GR.877159). Leave the road here and ride straight ahead and onto a track to Barrow. Turn right through the village of Barrow. At the T-junction (GR.895152), turn left to Market Overton. Take the first road turning on the left and follow this to the end. Cross the road going left then turn right, and take the track which is by the church (GR.886164). Follow this track to the end and then turn left keeping the hedge on the left and ride on to the woods.

Just before the woods, turn right and ride around the edge keeping the trees to the left. At the end of the woods turn right and continue alongside the edge

Wymondham Windmill.

of the hedge, keeping the hedge always on the left. Follow the hedge for about 1.50 miles as it twists and turns. After passing a house on the left, turn right along the hedge and at the end of the woods go left through a gap in the hedge. When the hedge ends, head for a barn and buildings which are straight ahead and, keeping them to the right, ride down a track to a road. *This road is The Viking Way.* Turn left and ride along the road, pass one right turn and then one turn on the left to take the next track to the left (GR.896201) and follow this track for 0.50 miles until it joins the green lane.

Turn right along the green lane and then immediately left, keeping the hedge on the left. Cross another bridleway at GR.883199. Continue to ride straight across fields to a metalled road (GR.865198). Turn right and ride along the road and then turn left at the top of the hill (GR.865200). Follow this road to a T-junction and turn left, then right at the next crossroads which is signed to Garthorpe and so return to your parking place.

TRAIL 10.

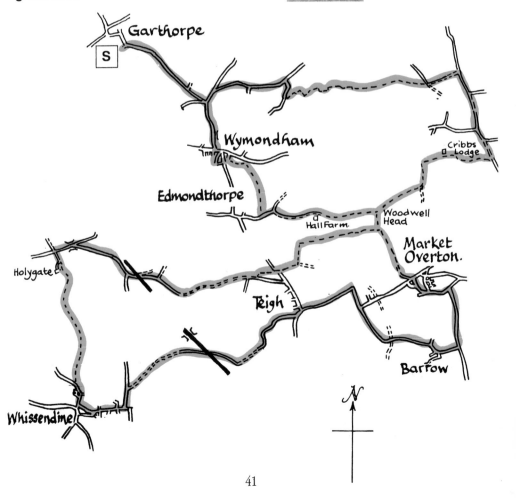

41

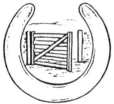

**A 18 MILE CIRCULAR TRAIL
(ANTI-CLOCKWISE)**

Ordnance Survey Maps:
Pathfinder: 855& 876
Landranger: 130

Parking & Starting Point:
Park on the road side, at the crossroads east of Waltham TV mast and Buckminster water tower. Start east of Waltham TV mast (GR.813234), on the Waltham on the Wolds to Garthorpe road.

Route Description:

Follow the 'field road' track from the crossroads, keeping the hedge on the right, to ride into the hollow; continue on, passing a building depot, and Waltham Lodge with its thatched roof on the right, to ride to the metalled road ahead (GR.804230).

Turn left opposite Waltham Lodge entrance, ride through the gate onto a metalled road and keep straight on to Waltham Pasture Farm. Before you reach the farm buildings turn sharp right (GR.809227) through gates keeping the hedge on the right until you reach the end of the field, then turn left with the hedge still on the right and, via a gate hook, go through the electric fence, to the gate at the bottom.

Keeping the hedge on the right, cross the stream and continue until you reach a small river. Follow the river to the end of the field, round the end and to the

left. *A short cut can be taken here by going straight on along the track past the maggot farm (GR.817216) on the right, onto the track and you will rejoin this route after paragraph five.* Turn right going over a ditch and stream. Keep to the right and go through a gate on the right and onto a track. Follow the track to the left, through Grange Farm to a metalled road (GR.807202). At the next gate before Freeby village, turn left through a further gate. Ride straight on through a narrow field and then go diagonally across a large grass field to the gate.

Follow the track keeping the hedge on the left, through the gap to the left and then, with the hedge on the right, ride until you reach an electric fence, passing through the fence via the gate hook. Continue straight on up to the houses at the top of the hill and through the electric fence gate and the gate on the left-hand side of the field to come to Saxby village.

Turn left at the metalled road (GR.819200) which leads to a stone track keeping the buildings of the maggot farm on the left (GR.817216). Cross the stream bridge, and turn right onto a grass track with the hedge on the right and continue through the gate at the end. Follow the track and cross the metalled road, (GR.823221) with the stream on the right. Turn right on a grassy track (GR.825224) with a wood on the left. Keep to the end of the field over the stream crossing. Go through the gate and straight on. Take the first turn on the right onto a grass track (GR.835229).

Follow the track down to the B676 at Coston and turn left, past the church on the left, and then turn right immediately over the bridge, turning left at the top of the hill (GR.853217) then left again, at Coston Lodge, and right onto the B676 towards Buckminster (GR.860223). Follow the road round a sharp right-hand bend, and in about 0.75 miles, a sharp bend left.

To shorten the ride here - turn left and then ride straight on to a stone track to Stonesby and return to your parking place as given in the last paragraph of this route description.

Go straight on to a green lane, (GR.869217). BEWARE here of deep ruts and holes. Go straight across a metalled road onto a stone track. *The TV mast is a visible landmark ahead to the left.* Pass the track to the left after the mast and keep straight on for 0.75 miles and then turn left on a stone track (GR.890199) to a metalled road then left again to Sewstern (GR.896202).

Ride straight through Sewstern village, and cross the B676, with Buckminster village to the left. Cross the next metalled road to a wide track leading to Buckminster Water Tower and The Viking Way.

Keep to the left hand track, The Viking Way, taking the steep slope down the grassy track which becomes a metalled road. In a few yards there is a hunting gate on the left. Ride through and follow

the track diagonally across an arable field towards Saltby Heath Farm and go through the electric fence by way of the hook and across to the farm road to continue on towards the wood. Go through the gate in the electric/wire fence onto a concrete road. Going straight through the corner of the wood, with wire fencing to your left, or right up the concrete road to Saltby Airfield. Turn left as the bridleway diverts round the edge of the airfield here.

Follow the concrete roadway to the end, until there is a line of fence posts in front. Go through the posts and turn left. Keeping the hedge on the left, follow the track down a steep hill to the edge of the quarry. At the next gateway ride across the middle of the field to the gate.

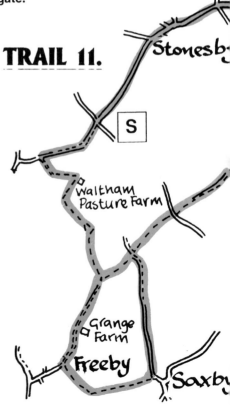

TRAIL 11.

44

Cross the metalled road (GR.854255) with Saltby village to the right. Take the grass track down hill using the bridge to cross the stream. With the hedge on the right go up the slope through arable fields to the gate onto a metalled road (GR.838250). Follow the road to the right to Stonesby.

Go through Stonesby village into the hollow, and take the left fork (GR.820244) up a steep hill passing farm buildings on the right, to the crossroads and the start of the ride.

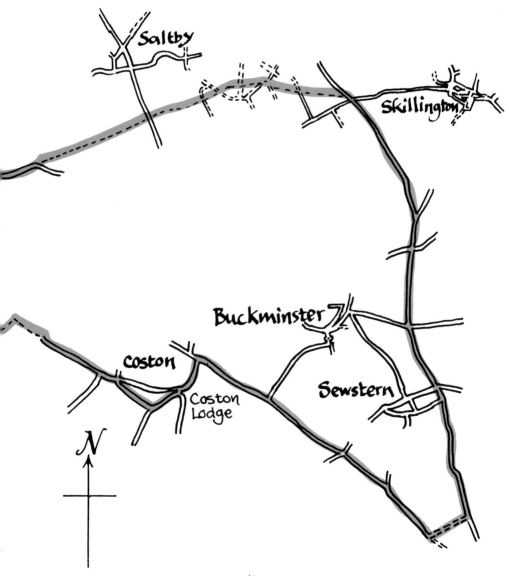

BRIDLEWAYS

HOW TO FIND YOURS

There are many miles of rights of way throughout the country on which you may ride: these fall into three types: they are Bridleways, Byways Open to All Traffic and Unclassified County Roads (which may be referred to as field roads or green lanes).

MAPS

The best maps to use while riding are the Ordnance Survey 1:25,000 (2.5" to the mile) Maps since these show the field boundaries. The maps of this scale, known as the Pathfinder Series, show Bridleways as a line of green dashes.

The Rights of Way information shown on a printed map was correct at the time that the map was printed but changes do take place: if you have any reason to query the Rights of Way information on a printed map it will be necessary for you to consult the Definitive Map and the County Council Rights of Way Officer to resolve the query.

The Definitive Map is a legal document held and maintained by the County Council; copies may also be found at County Council Area/Local/Divisional Offices and Parish Clerks' Offices and local libraries. The Definitive Maps are available for inspection by any member of public who wishes to see them. It would be a courtesy to telephone and ask for the relevant sheets to be made available.

**THE BRITISH
HORSE SOCIETY**

A 18 MILE CIRCULAR TRAIL
(CLOCKWISE)

Ordnance Survey Maps:
Pathfinder: 854 & 855
Landrangers: 129 &130

Parking & Starting Point:
Parking is available on the roadside at crossroads east of the Waltham TVmast (GR.813234) on the Waltham-on-Wolds to Garthorpe road. This is also your starting point.

Route Description:

Follow the 'field road' track from the crossroads, keeping the hedge on the right at first, passing Waltham Lodge with its thatched roof, on the right, to come to the metalled road and a T-junction at Freeby Lane (GR.802230).

Turn right up Freeby Lane keeping Pedigree Petfoods to the right, to the A607. Turn right again, into Waltham-on-the-Wolds, which is not such a busy road. Take the first turn left into Moor Leys Lane. At the end of the track take the left hand gate into an arable field. Keep straight on with the hedge on the right and ride across to the handgate and posts in the opposite hedge. The handgate is to the right of a small spinney. Cross the ditch, by way of the bridge, and ride straight across the field to the handgate in the opposite hedge. (GR.789232).

At GR.789232 follow the line of the bridleway by keeping the hedge on the

right all the way to Thorpe Hindles farmhouse. Take the left turn on the grass track onto a cinder track, and go right on the cinder track over a concrete bridge and up through the farm buildings to Scalford back road and Melton Spinney (GR.768222).

Turn right towards Scalford, keeping the houses and farms on your right, and pass between the walls of the dismantled railway bridge. Turn right towards Wycomb, with Scalford village to the left and the farm and shooting range to the right, and go under the old railway bridge. Take the first left through Wycomb village, and follow the road past the isolated house on the left.

At the end of the next field turn left keeping the stonewall on your right. *Goadby Marwood village is to the right.* Follow the track down through the cutting and along the small embankment, to go through the gate and then sharp uphill to bear left through the gate onto the field track. Follow to Bellemere Farm and in front of the farm follow the metalled road to meet the Salford to Eastwell road (GR.761263) to turn right here.

Pass Piper Hole Farm on your left and turn right along the road and continue for 0.75 miles to go through the gate and turn right down the track, keeping the hedge on the left (GR.765272).

Continue until you come to two gates in front of you and taking the right-hand gate, go through and follow the track to the metalled road at White Lodge (GR.784273).

With White Lodge Farm on the left, and keeping the bridge to the left, cross straight over the road and take the bridleway which goes diagonally across the paddocks which lie behind the farm. Ride towards the far corner of the field, go through two hunting gates and then, with the hedge on the left, turn left through the next gate and cross the old railway line. Ride downhill to the handgate and bridge in the bottom, left hand corner of the field. Go through the hunting gate and turn left keeping the trees and stream on the left. Pass through two fields and at the far side of the second field, turn right and ride uphill, with the hedge on your left, to a gate which you go through to meet the metalled road (GR.795283).

Go left at the road and turn immediately right onto the track. Keeping the hedge on the left ride on down to Bottom Farmhouse. *The track is behind the house and goes through the garden so please be considerate.* Carry on along the track until you meet the metalled road where you turn left to Eaton Grange, and ride along until you meet the Eaton to Branston road.

Turn right at the road junction and follow the road into Branston village where you turn right for Knipton, leaving the Wheel Inn on your left. *This is a good lunch stop!* In 0.50 miles the road bends sharp left; here take the track which goes to the right and follow through to Croxton Kerrial passing the sewage works in the hollow.

In Croxton Kerrial, turn right, then with a grass field and church to the left, turn left and then right again to meet the A607 (GR.838292). CROSS A607 WITH CARE and ride towards Saltby. In approximately 1.25 miles you will come to Swallow Hole Wood on the right.

Turn right down the far side of the wood and follow the track through to Green Lane and go straight on to the stone track called Mary Lane. You will pass Croxton Park to the right and Bescaby Farm to the left. Ride on until you come to the metalled road. Follow the road through to Waltham on the Wolds.

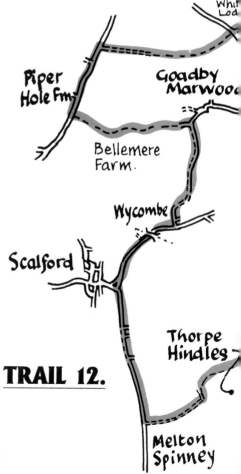

TRAIL 12.

48

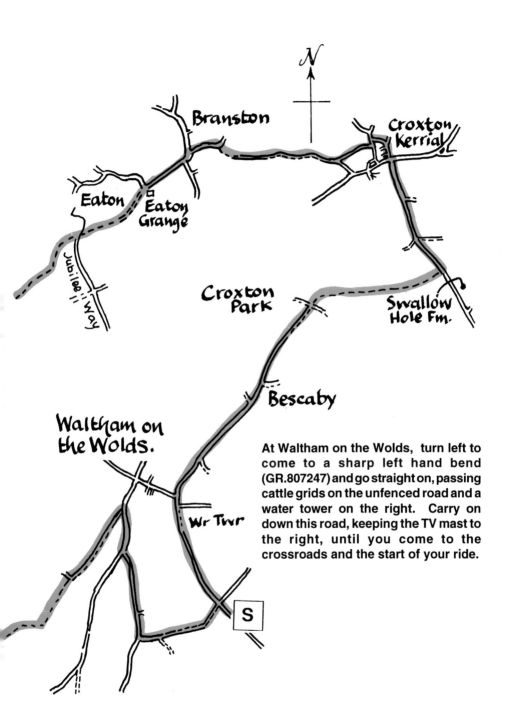

At Waltham on the Wolds, turn left to come to a sharp left hand bend (GR.807247) and go straight on, passing cattle grids on the unfenced road and a water tower on the right. Carry on down this road, keeping the TV mast to the right, until you come to the crossroads and the start of your ride.

BELVOIR

TRAIL 13

A 17 MILE CIRCULAR TRAIL (ANTI-CLOCKWISE)

Ordnance Survey Maps:
Pathfinders: 834, 835 & 855
Landrangers: 129 & 130

Parking & Starting Point:
Parking is available at Saltby Church crossroads (GR.851265).

Route Description:

Leave your parking place and Saltby Church on the left and follow the Wyville road. In 0.25 miles turn right onto a track, keeping the hedge on the left and passing the wood which is also on the left. At the end of the wood follow the track to the right, round a grassy mound and then continue to Saltby Airfield. Find the track towards a gate in the wire fence. This follows the perimeter of the disused airfield. There is a hunting gate to the left side of a gate by a wood.

Ride along the track and keep going straight on until you come to a hunting gate at the far end of fields. Go through the gate and onto the grassy track. This is The Viking Way (GR.875270), and the signpost is to the right on this track. Turn left from the gate and go along The Viking Way until you meet the metalled road.

Continue straight on at the road for a short way, keeping straight on where the road turns sharp right and back

onto the track - The Viking Way. Go straight over the next metalled road at The Three Queens Public House and past Hill Top Farm to the right, and on up to meet the A607 (GR.854306). CARE there can be fast traffic here.

Cross straight over the A607 and onto the track, with the wood on the right and farm to the left. This section may

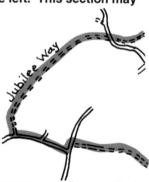

be boggy. When you meet the metalled road, go straight on over and onto Sewstern Lane. This is still the Viking Way. Keep on until you come to the next road junction at Brewers Grave (GR.846337).

With the iron gates to the left, *these are at the former main entrance to Belvoir Castle, dating back to when very long drives were fashionable,* **cross straight over the metalled road and follow the track straight on going under an old railway bridge and over a canal bridge. Take the next track to the left, this is still The Viking Way, and follow the track under the next railway bridge, and over another canal bridge** - *the Dirty Duck pub is on the right* - **and so on to the metalled road junction (GR.839350).**

TRAIL 13.

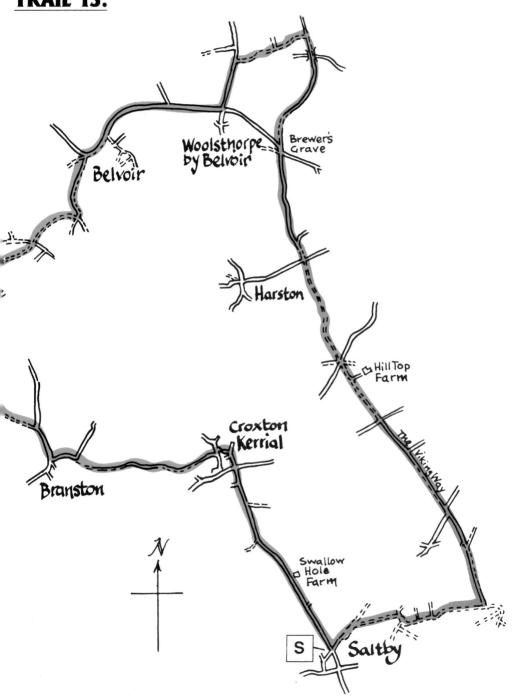

At the road junction, turn left towards Woolsthorpe, and at the next crossroads, *where you will see the old Belvoir Hunt stables on the right,* turn right towards Belvoir Castle (GR.838343). Follow the road round the castle grounds, keeping the car park and castle grounds to the left, and past the wood on the right.

At GR.815328 turn right onto a track up the hill, past Reeded Cottage on the right. Cross straight over the track and go into the woods. Follow the track through the woods, keeping to the main track, which is The Jubilee Way, until you meet the metalled road (GR.790305). Turn left here and go uphill on the road and then right, on a corner, back onto The Jubilee Way.

When you reach the end of the track turn left into Tofts Lane and follow the track until it meets the metalled road. Turn left on the road, then immediately right onto a track that takes you down to the metalled road turning right into Branston.

In Branston, pass The Wheel Inn on your right and take the left turn (GR.810295) towards Knipton. In about 0.50 miles, the uphill road bends sharp left. Take the track to the right and follow it through to Croxton Kerrial, passing the sewage works in the hollow.

When you reach Croxton Kerrial; turn right, then left, keeping the field and the church to the left, then turn right again to the A607. Cross over the A607 (GR.838291), past Swallow Hole Wood on the right and the farmhouse on the left to arrive at Saltby Church and the start of your ride.

Belvoir Castle.

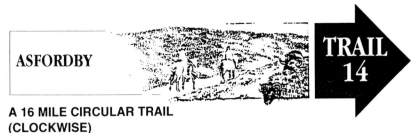

A 16 MILE CIRCULAR TRAIL (CLOCKWISE)

Ordnance Survey Maps:
Pathfinder: 854 & 875
Lamdranger: 129

Parking & Starting Points:
Parking is available on the good grass verge south of Carlton Lodge Farm (GR.689138), Gaddesby Lane, Gaddesby. This is due north of the village. Your ride starts from here.

Route Description:

From your parking place, ride north past Carlton Lodge Farm (GR.689138) and take the signed bridleway to the left (GR.688141). Follow the old lane through a handgate and into an arable field with a hedge on the left and then ride along an overgrown track between two hedges and go through a waymarked gate. Ride down a wide grass farm track with a small wood on the left, then up the side of an arable field with the hedge on the left. *This track is waymarked.* Do not follow the track to the right to Messenger Lodge Farm, but continue straight ahead through a small waymarked gate. Cross a grass field leaving the farm buildings to the right. Ride through a waymarked gate and then continue on towards Brooksby with the hedge on the left. Go through a marked gateway and onto a hard track passing Spinney Farm cottages on the right.

On meeting the main road (GR.673159), CROSS WITH CARE and continue towards Hoby leaving Brooksby Agricultural College buildings to the left. Cross over the River Wreake and continue to Hoby. *The Blue Bell makes an excellent lunch stop in Hoby.* Ride on through the village around many bends and turn right at the end to Frisby. Ride along the road for 20 yards and turn onto the signed bridleway to the left (GR.671178), which lies through a metal gate. Ride diagonally to the top left corner of the grass field to a handgate. Go through the handgate and continue straight on with the hedge on the left to ride over the bridge with the white concrete posts. At the end of the field, go through the handgate and onto an overgrown track - you may need to ride in single file just here. Ride along to, and through, a small copse then proceed to the top right corner of the field to a handgate. Go through the handgate, which has weights attached, and continue to ride across the next field to go through a gateway leaving Barn Farm to the right.

After crossing one more grass field, go through a handgate and into another overgrown track with a hedge and ditch on the right. At the end of this track go through the metal gate into a grass field and through the next gate to continue down the left-hand side of a large poultry house to come to a new metal gate. Go through the gate onto a hard track and in about 50 yards go through the next metal gate and onto a road (GR.681200). CARE HERE,

53

visibility is restricted to 100 yards in both directions. Turn left onto the road using the good verge and after 50 yards turn right and cross over to Shoby village.

Follow this pretty metalled lane into Grimston. At the T-junction, turn right with the Black Horse Public House on the left and ride towards the end of the village where you take the signed bridleway to the left (GR.687218) through The Lilacs farmyard and out into a grass field. Follow the yellow marker posts passing Grimston Gorse, Barn Farm and Saxelby Wood all to your left, to meet a metalled road at GR.696224. Cross straight over, going through a handgate and follow the hard track which is waymarked to Wartnaby. In Wartnaby follow the road round to the right going through a wooden handgate to the left-hand side of a private driveway. *The bridleway from Wartnaby to Saxelby has recently been diverted so is not as shown on Ordnance Survey maps.* Follow the signs and waymarks until you pass through a small copse where you rejoin the Ordnance Survey mapped route. The remainder of bridleway is clearly marked to the metalled road (GR.702211).

Turn left onto the road, go up hill to a T-junction, turn left and soon after turn right onto a bridleway (GR.707212). *This bridleway has been diverted to the north to avoid a coal mine, it has been clearly marked and well maintained by National Coal.* Follow the signs to meet Welby Lane. Turn right and proceed southwards passing over the mine which gives an excellent view of its workings.

Continue on this road until you pass under a railway arch. A few yards beyond there is a road crossing with a barrier and you will see the bridleway straight ahead on the other side of the road (GR.719193). Go left for a few yards to avoid the barrier and then cross the road, which is not too busy as Asfordby now has a by-pass, then proceed along the grass verge to a wooden gate and bridlepath. Follow this along an old grass track, through a gate into a stone track where a dairy herd passes daily. Keep going south along the track through two more gates and into an arable field. Follow the fence to the right, cutting the corner of the field, and go towards a gate ahead (GR.721181).

Go through the gate and into a grass field, over an old bridge and follow the old flood bank to the right through a handgate and onto the bridge over the River Wreake. *Look to your right for a lovely view of the river and Kirby Bellars church.* Turn left at the top of the lane into Kirby Bellars village street and continue southwards crossing the main Leicester road (GR.716176) WITH CARE. *The easiest way to cross the road is to go left, then right: there are good verges and visibility.* Follow this small metalled road south towards Gaddesby. After 1.25 miles there is a bridleway signed to the left.

Here you may choose your route. EITHER:

a) *If your horse still has some energy this is a very pretty route with excellent views of the new Quorn Hunt Kennels.* Follow the grass track with the hedge on the right, along the edge of a large field. *The new Quorn Hunt Kennels are to the left.* The grass track continues after the first gateway with a

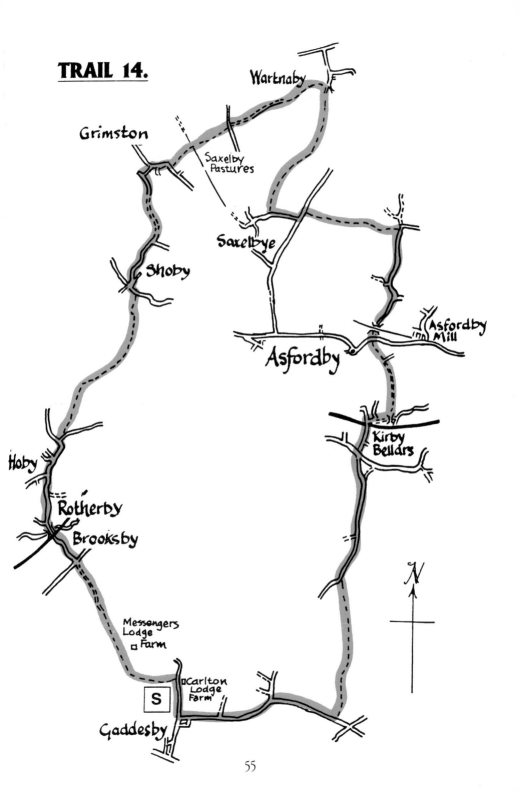

TRAIL 14.

Wartnaby

Grimston

Saxelby
Pastures

Saxelbye

Shoby

Asfordby
Mill

Asfordby

Hoby

Kirby
Bellars

Rotherby

Brooksby

Messengers
Lodge
Farm

Carlton
Lodge
Farm

S

Gaddesby

N

hedge on the left. Cross over one arable field then along the edge of two more fields with the hedge on the left until you meet a grass track. Turn left on the track, ride to the corner of a wood and go right, through the handgate and follow the edge of the wood on the left until you meet a metalled road (GR.714135). Turn right on this road and then left at the T-junction and follow the road to Gaddesby. At the T-junction, turn right and return to your parking place.

OR:

b) If your horse is tired, you can follow the metalled road for just over two miles to Gaddesby. Just north of the village, turn right at the T-junction into Gaddesby Lane and ride along the lane to your parking point.

Asfordby Mine.

HUNGARTON & BARKBY

A 15 MILE CIRCULAR TRAIL (ANTI-CLOCKWISE)

Ordnance Survey Maps:
Landranger: 140 & 141
Pathfinder: 895 & 875

Parking & Starting Point:
Parking is available on the good, wide verges in Enderby Lane, between Sludge Hall Farm and the village of Cold Newton (GR.719056), 1.75 miles north-west of Tilton-on-the-Hill.

Information for Alternative Parking and Starting Point:
If you are coming from the north of the county you may prefer to start your ride from the northern point GR.668102. Parking is available on the verges on Ridgemore Lane, Queniborough, between New York Farm and the sharp bend where the road goes up to South Croxton (GR.663105 and GR.668102). Ridgemore Lane runs east-west from the Barkby Road going from Queniborough to South Croxton. From your parking place ride to the sharp bend (GR.668102) and take the bridleway following it down the side of the field. Ride right across this field and also the second field to a bridlegate in the middle of a hedge. Go through the bridlegate and head for a signpost at the road which lies ahead. On meeting the road, turn right onto Barkby Holt Lane and follow the ride description from * point. When the described ride ends, you will continue to follow the route from the beginning, returning to your own parking place when you reach * again.

Route Description:
From your parking place in Enderby's Lane, ride south, up the steep hill past Sludge Hall Farm and Lord Morton's Covert to the crossroads. Turn left onto a small road. *CARE, at certain times of the day, this can be busy but there is good visibility.* Follow the road for about 800 yards and look for a sign on the right and pointing to a wooden farm gate in the hedge, on your left opposite the gate, there is a red triangular road sign marked 'Gate'. Go through the gate and continue along the track heading for the metal gate which is in the hedgerow diagonally across the corner of the grass field. Go through this gate then head straight for an old, static, removal van that is used for storage, following the old track which is just visible on the ground. Just before you come to the removal van, (GR.733058), turn sharp left and follow the rutted track keeping the hedge on your left and ride down the hill to Hamner's Lodge Farm. Ride through the farm yard using the narrow bridlegate between a wooden hut and some large metal gates. *If cattle are loose in the yard, please take care to see they do not follow you through the gate!*

Continue to ride on down the steep hill, over the brook and through two metal gates onto a metalled road. The road ends at a T-junction on the Lowesby to Cold Newton Estate road. Cross straight over this road and take the bridleway (GR.719068), going through a wooden farm gate. Bear left in the first field to a bridlegate in the bottom left hand corner. Go through the gate and after crossing the brook, go left up the next field and down to a bridge. Cross the bridge and bear left up the next field to a blue and white gate which is near a water trough. Ride left over the next field to come to the road at the side of a spinney. *White's Barn House is to the left.*

Cross over the road and ride through the spinney. *The track is very narrow here so you should ride in single file.*

When you come to the bridlegate, go through and into a grass field. Go straight across the field to a farm gate, going through the gate and across the farm drive. Ride diagonally across the next field, which often has horses in it, then ride across two fields and follow the waymarks into the track lying straight ahead through a gate into a tree-lined avenue. *You are now in Baggrave Park, which until recently was the home of Asil Nadir.* Continue straight ahead along the concrete road through Waterloo Lodge Farm riding straight between the barns. Ride straight ahead across the field following the tractor tracks and tracks left by previous users, to come to a metalled road (GR.680092).

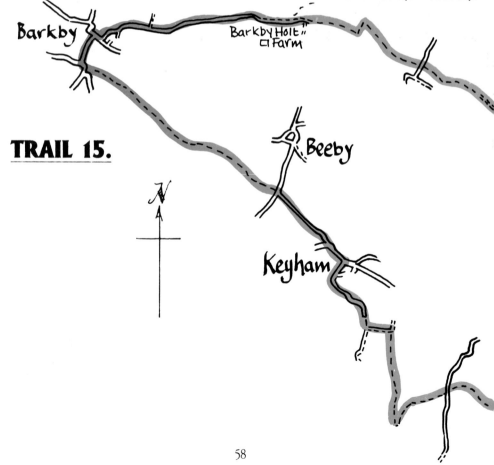

TRAIL 15.

58

Cross straight over the road into a track, keeping the hedge on your left and ride into Barkby Holt Wood. In the wood stay on the main track as it bears left and then right to avoid possible mud. Once out of the wood, continue along the track which becomes Barkby Holt Lane and takes you into Barkby village.

If you used the alternative parking at the northern end of the trail, you will finish your ride here by leaving the track soon after the wood via a bridleway to the right, opposite Barkby Holt Farm (GR.664098). This bridleway will take you to and from your parking place in the lane.*

Ride into Barkby village and at the T-junction in the village turn right and then left into Thorpe Lane. Immediately before the Barkby Thorpe village sign, look left to find an unmarked bridlegate leading onto a track (GR.636092). Go through this gate and along the narrow

track to the field. Ride straight across the field with the hedge on your left until you reach the far end of the spinney. Go through the gate on your left to pick up a track on the other side of the hedge. Ride on to beyond the second spinney on the right and go through a gate so that the hedge is again on the left as you ride through one field to come to a gateway. *There are marvellous views from here.*

Ride through the gateway so that the hedge is now on the right and continue on to come to a road (GR.660075). Go through the gate and cross Scraptoft Lane into Keyham Lane and continue to ride on the road for 0.75 miles to take the first right-hand turning signposted to Keyham. *There is a nice Public House on the left - The Dog & Gun - where you might like to take a lunch break.* Ride straight ahead in the village, signposted 'Dead End', and go through the Kennels taking the left-hand gate to leave their yard. Continue to follow the lane to a bridge leading into a field. Go over the bridge and keep right along the hedge to a cattle pen with two gates (GR.672057). Ride through the cattle pen and then turn left up the hill. At the top, go through the double metal gates, which are often open, and turn right immediately along the other side of the hedge heading for a field gate onto a bridge over the disused railway line.

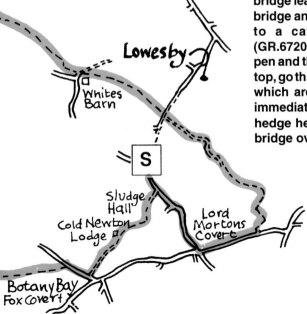

Continue riding straight ahead, crossing four fields. In the field with four gates, take the gate by the water trough, which has a dead tree lying beyond it. When you meet the grass track, turn left onto the Unclassified County Road and follow this route until you meet the gate at GR677046. Here you follow the red arrow signpost diagonally left down the hill for two fields to a metalled road (GR.683049), passing Monk's Grave, which is a Motte, on your left. At the road, turn left then take the marked bridleway which lies almost immediately on the right through a farm gate. Ride up the hill to meet the Unclassified County Road at the top. Turn right and follow the track for 1.25 miles passing Botany Bay and **Billesdon Coplow**, *this is a very famous Quorn Hunt covert*, **on the right and on to meet a metalled road (GR.707049).**

Turn right along the road and after 350 yards take the bridleway to the left along a stone track leading to Cold Newton Lodge. Go through the farm gate and into the farm yard then turn immediately sharp left through a red gate with a white top into a field. Keep the hedge on the right and follow it around the farm house and continue to ride straight through the gate into an arable field ignoring the bridleway to the left, north of the farm house. You will now come to Cold Newton Lodge. Pass the Lodge on your right and take the drive out to join Enderby's Lane and so return to your parking place.

Billesdon Coplow.

BURLEY ON THE HILL

TRAIL 16

A 19 MILE CIRCULAR TRAIL (ANTI-CLOCKWISE)

Ordnance Survey Maps:
Landranger: 129, 130 & 141
Pathfinder: 875, 876, 895 & 896

Parking & Starting Point:
Parking is available half way between Ashwell and Oakham, in a large lay-by outside the Kennels (GR.866114) or on the road between Langham and Burley, between the railway crossing and the cross roads (GR.863110).

Route Description:

From either parking place, proceed to the crossroads at GR.866110 and take the road due east to Burley and ride along here for 0.75 miles. Take the signed bridleway to the left (GR.878107) to Whissendine. The track to Whissendine is 3.50 miles long and bears left across a field to a very dirty gateway, go through the gate and into a grass field. Ride diagonally across to an iron gate in a wire fence to the next grass field. Go through the gate and towards the next gate. Turn right before the gate and follow the old wooden fence line on the left to the top of the field and go straight on through a large wooden gate into a small paddock. Cross this paddock to a handgate and concrete bridge into a lane. Cross the Oakham road (GR.866123), which is small but busy, with good visibility, and go into a dirt lane.

Cross over the railway line, which is still used, and follow the pretty grass lane to a metal gate where you take a narrow track to the right (GR.861124).

Do not continue straight ahead through the gate as this is a footpath. **Follow the track uphill to Larch Wood to meet a small metalled road (GR.856128). Turn right and immediately left down a tree lined grass track.** *This track affords good views of the Vale of Catmose on both sides. To the left you can see the television mast which you will pass later on towards the end of the ride and also Langham Church.* **Go through the gate, along the edge of an arable field, then back onto a grass track and out into an arable field with a hedge to the left.** *You can now see Waltham TV mast to the right.*

At the end of the field you will meet a track coming from the left. Turn right (GR.838128)on this track keeping the hedge on the left and follow this lovely grass track down the hill into Whissendine. Go through the gate onto a metalled road (GR.836137), turn left and follow the road into the village. *Note the smart square tower of Whissendine Church to the left.*

Follow the village street to the bottom of the hill and the White Lion Public House. Then cross the bridge and take the first turn left and follow the back road through the village keeping the brook on the left to a T-junction (GR.825142).

Turn left on to a quiet road then right

61

(GR.825140) at the end of the village down a small, sheltered country road signed to Cold Overton. *Here there are excellent verges and an old windmill to the right.* When you meet the main road, A606 (*CARE, there is very good visibility in both directions*), turn left and ride for a few yards along the grass verge towards Oakham, then take the first turn right (GR.813127) onto a gated road signed to Cold Overton. Follow this pretty little road through North Field Farm then Cold Overton Grange on the right and soon after take the signed bridleway to the left (GR.809109) just before some trees and a bridge over the brook. *This bridleway may show as footpath on your Ordnance Survey map.*

Ride towards the metal gate with a horseshoe on it and turn right before the gate with the wire fence on the left and follow the fence to the top of the hill, to a yellow finger post. Cross an arable field straight down hill to a yellow finger post at the bottom. Cross the brook via the sleeper bridge. Turn right and follow the track with the hedge on the right around the edge of an

TRAIL 16

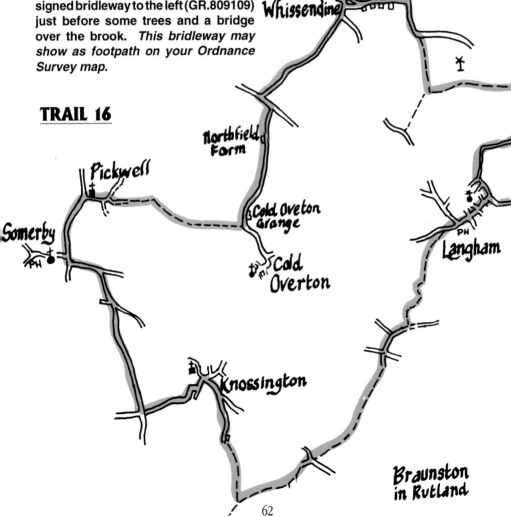

arable field, uphill to meet a concrete road. *If it is very wet, the concrete road is an Unclassified County Road (GR.797111), and if you turn left on it and follow it bearing right as it becomes a dirt track, it will take you into Pickwell village.*

Turn right over the bridge and immediately left up the side of an arable field with a brook on the left to a yellow finger post at the top. Cross the fence line then turn left and follow the headland track with the hedge on the left to a Radio Hut and mast. Pass well to the right of these to avoid numerous wires, into a farm track going down hill to Pickwell village.

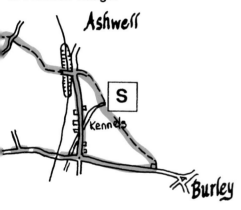

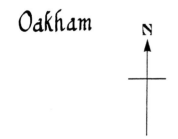

Turn left on the metal road through the village and left at the T-junction (GR.784113) onto the Somerby road. Do not go into the village of Somerby but carry straight on and take the first left to Cold Overton (GR.782104) and take the first right hand turn to Knossington and Braunston. After 500 yards, bear right (GR.788098) after the Council Tip into a gated road and follow this to a crossroads. Turn left (GR.792080) to Knossington. Follow the road up hill into the village then go right at the T-junction and take the first turn right to Braunston. After 300 yards, at the bottom of the hill, turn right through a wooden gate on the right of the house, into a lane. This bridleway is not always signed (GR.804083). Go through the wooden gate at the top and down across a grass field on the other side. Go through another wooden gate, over the River Gwash and up the grass track to the other side. At GR.806067 you meet a marked bridleway coming from the right. Turn left onto this and follow the grass track with the hedge on the right. Go through the gap in the hedge and bear slightly right to continue down the track with hedge on the left, turn left with the grass track when you reach the bottom of the field and the hedge is now on the right.

At the end of the field continue on the bridleway (GR.813069). Ride through the handgate and cross a small field bearing slightly left to go through a metal gate in the corner to enter the next field. Keeping 100 yards to the left of the hedgerow, follow down to a metal gate and a muddy ford. Cross the ford, which has a firm bottom, and continue up the lane to a road (GR.818073). Cross over into a marked bridleway riding diagonally across the first field and through a handgate. Ride across the second field and through another handgate and into an overgrown track. Pass the junction with Braunston Bridleway (GR.825079) and ride out into a grass field. *The Aerial Tower on the Oakham-Knossington Road comes into view. This is what you could see early on in the ride from the Vale of Catmose to the north.*

Follow the track through a metal gate to meet the Cold Overton road. Cross over onto a tarmac track and continue over a cattle grid after 300 yards. Turn left through the next metal gate onto an unmarked bridleway (GR.834093). Follow the left hedge round and go through the second unmarked gate on the left and turn right following the grass track with the hedge on the right, heading for the wood. Follow the track

round to the left of the woods and then down towards Langham with the hedge on the right, through two gates to join the metal road (GR.840108). Turn right into Langham. Carry straight on following the main road for a few yards then a small village road to Burley and take the left hand turn to Ashwell on the last right hand bend in the village (GR.846112).

Follow this beautiful country road for 1.50 miles to Larch Wood on the right at the top of a hill (GR.856128). Turn right on the bridleway immediately after the wood and retrace your footsteps back to your parking place. *If you have parked in the lay-by on the Langham to Burley road, it would be quicker to continue on the Burley road for one mile to your parking place.*

St. Andrews Church, Whissendine.

MELTON MOWBRAY ROUND

TRAIL 17

A 20 MILE CIRCULAR TRAIL (ANTI-CLOCKWISE)

Ordnance Survey Maps:
Pathfinder: 854 & 875
Landranger: 129

Parking & Starting Point:
Parking is available on the grass verge in a quiet lane between Wartnaby and the B676 and also between Wartnaby and Ab Kettleby (GR.715232).

Route Description:

Leave your parking place and ride into Wartnaby village. **Pass the church on the left hand side and go through the five-barred gate immediately in front of you at a place where an Unclassified County Road branches off to the left. Follow the waymarked route and ride due south towards Saxelbye village.** *This is a very pretty bridleway which goes over grassland, through a wood, and on to pass Wartnaby fish ponds.* **Turn left at the end of the bridleway and ride up the hill to Glebe Farm. Turn left at the top and then right onto the byway (GR.708211) which goes to Asfordby Mine.** *This road has been diverted by the Coal Board, but where it begins is obvious to the rider.* **Follow this well marked route, until you meet the lane. Turn right here (GR.722209) and follow to Asfordby Valley.**

At Asfordby Valley you will meet the A6006. *CARE this is a very busy road.* **Cross this road and take the bridleway to Kirby Bellars. This joins an** Unclassified County Road in Kirby Bellars which leads to the main street where you turn left. Follow the road to the A607 to cross (GR.717176) WITH CARE, and go down the lane opposite towards Gaddesby heading south. **Look out for the 'New Quorn Hunt Kennels' on your left and take the bridleway (GR.713156) from there to Ashby Pastures. At the end of the bridleway turn left and then go left at the crossroads. Ride straight over the next crossroads to turn left when you come to the T-junction on the outskirts of Great Dalby (GR.739145). Just past 'March House' and before the old railway, take the unmarked track on the right (GR.738155) and follow it to the next unmarked bridleway across an arable field and so not always obvious to the rider. Ride along this bridleway to leave it by turning right at GR.742175 just north of 'Old Guadaloupe'.**

Follow this road over two crossroads and then turn right onto the A606 taking the next unmarked track on your left. When you come to the crossroads of tracks (GR.771174), turn left and follow this Unclassified County Road to meet the B676. *The railway is crossed both here and at Kirby Bellars, by a road bridge.* Cross straight over here taking special CARE as the opposite road is slightly staggered and there is poor visibility and sometimes fast traffic.

Ride along this road to the village of Thorpe Arnold to cross the A607

(GR.770201) onto an Unclassified County Road. *This runs along the course of the footpath shown on the map.* At the end of the Unclassified County Road, turn right (GR.768211) onto the lane and ride to Scalford. Go straight through the village heading towards Melton Mowbray. *Ride with care on the lane leading from Scalford village as it is very winding.* After the old railway and cemetery, turn right onto a very quiet lane. *There are also private driveways on the right but the lane comes last and is quite obvious.*

TRAIL 17

Continue along this lane past Grange Farm and The Willows. Turn left at the next T-junction and turn right at the following T-junction to ride straight through Holwell village. After the last house in the village and just before the next T-junction, take the unmarked bridleway on the left which goes across an arable field.

When you reach the end of this bridleway you will meet the A606 (GR.726232). Turn left, with CARE, onto the A606 and ride along the road for a short distance and turn right opposite the public house and go into Ab Kettleby village. *You may see Desert Orchid who lives in a paddock on the right at the edge of the village.* Keep straight on this road and follow it back to Wartnaby and your starting point.

66

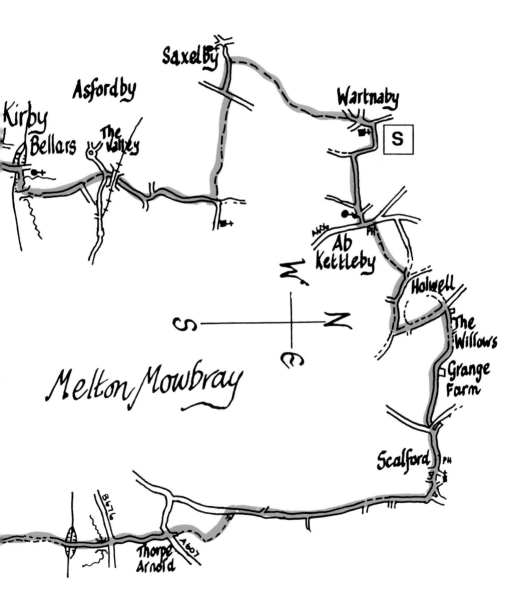

Saxelby

Asfordby

Wartnaby

Kirby
Bellars

The
Valley

S

Ab
Kettleby

Holwell

The
Willows

Melton Mowbray

Grange
Farm

Scalford

Thorpe
Arnold

The Old Rectory

Belton-in-Rutland,
Uppingham, Rutland. LE15 9LE
Tel: 0572 86279   Fax: 0572 86343

*Late 19th Century rectory &
annexe in 14 acres, overlooking
the Eye Brook Valley
and
rolling Rutland Countryside.*

Excellent bridleways.

Bed & Breakfast.

Stabling/Grazing.

*Also self catering
accommodation.*

*Trail guides available
if required.*

Open all year

TRAIL GUIDE

for routes
**1, 2, 4, 5, 7,
9, 14, 15, 18 & 19**

Experienced horsewoman

Excellent knowledge
of Countryside

Can arrange
accommodation and
hire of horses if required

Contact:
Mrs. Alex Pyper
Tel: 085 889 620

High Holme, Hallaton, Market Harborough,
Leicestershire LE16 8UD

LGF - Livery Yard

Lower Grange Farm, Gibsons Lane,
Dalby Wolds, Leics. LE14 3LH

we offer:

Bed & Breakfast Accommodation
1 double & 1single room here with
another 4 rooms available locally.

Evening meal by prior arrangement

Stabling (depending on season)
for at least 6-8 horses with
grazing by arrangement

An all weather outdoor manége
which is floodlit

Access to a cross country course
$1/2$ mile away (at extra charge)

Contact:

Sue Fox
Tel: 0664 823640

FOLLOWING A ROUTE

The descriptions given in this
book were correct at the time of
printing but it should be borne in
mind that landmarks and
conditions can change.
It is assumed every user will
carry and be competent in the
use of the appropriate Ordnance
Survey Pathfinder or
Landranger map. This is
essential as the route may not
be waymarked along the whole
of its length.

FEARN FARM

TRAIL 18

A 16 MILE CIRCULAR TRAIL (ANTI-CLOCKWISE)

Ordnance Survey Maps:
Pathfinder: 916, 917, 895 & 896
Landranger: 141

Parking & Starting Point:
Parking is available by prior arrangement with Mrs Summers at Fearn Farm, telephone (0858) 89285. Fearn Farm is situated 1 mile south-west of the Allexton turn off the A47 (GR.801986)

Route Description:

Leaving Fearn Farm, (GR.801986), proceed southwards down the farm driveway and go straight across the Allexton road, through double gates and onto an Unclassified County Road to Horninghold. *This is not marked on the Ordnance Survey maps.* Pass through a farm yard and ride on into the village. Turn right at the T-junction (GR.807971) and ride up the hill. When you reach the top of the hill take the left hand turn to Blaston. Ride through the park and on leaving turn left and proceed through the very pretty village of Blaston which is still almost entirely privately owned. As the road bends to the right out of the village, take the left hand fork (GR.811958) onto a track, bearing right onto the bridleway which goes uphill on the headland to meet a quiet road at the top (GR.823968).

Turn left to leave the road at the left-hand bend and ride straight ahead through double gates. Do not follow the bridleway sign, but take the Unclassified County Road that goes due north keeping the hedge to your left. *This is not marked on the Ordnance Survey maps.* Keep on this road until you meet the fence, where you go through the farm gate to the right of a small bridlegate and ride straight on down the hill to Knob Hill Farm. *Take care on entering the farm, there are many wonderful fowl running in the yard and the Guinea Fowl could well startle your horse!* Leave the farm and cross the road (GR.820980) continuing northwards through the gate opposite, *again not marked on the Ordnance Survey maps.* Ride along the clearly marked track through four gates passing Allexton Wood to your right, until you come to a T-junction with a lane (GR.815996).

Turn right and continue down the hill through the tiny hamlet of Allexton, where you will cross the A47 (GR.819007). *CARE, cross with caution; although the visibility is good, this is a fast and busy road.* On reaching the other side, turn right and proceed for 250 yards along a wide grass verge until you reach a lay-by with a handgate in the hedge (GR.823005) and a marked bridleway. Follow this lovely grass track which steadily climbs upward, then goes steeply down the other side to cross a brook, only to climb again steeply all the way to Ridlington.

On meeting the metalled road (GR.848027), turn left and ride along

TRAIL 18

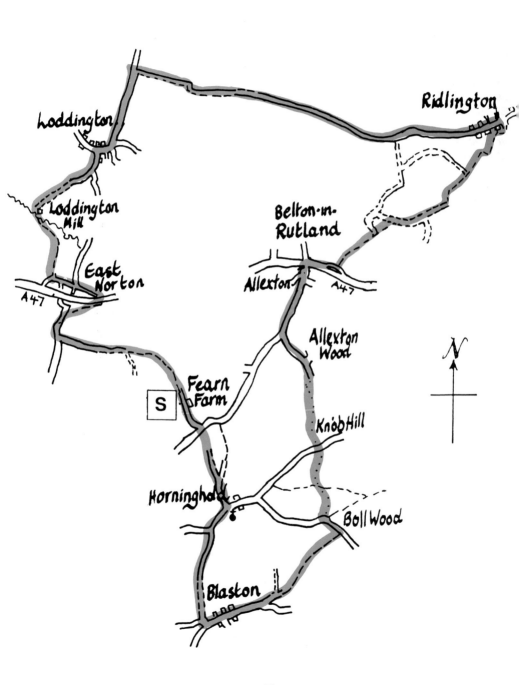

the track. *The views here are fantastic and you will feel as if you are riding on top of the world as you look across high Leicestershire and beyond Melton Mowbray to your right and your return route to the left.* **Cross two bridleways and at the second crossing be careful to take the correct gate - do not go left as this will take you down the hill to Belton.** *If you are on the correct route, shortly after passing through the gate you will pass a Trig. point at 191 metres. (GR.808032).*

Ride past the large wood to your right and cross through four fields keeping straight on to a track which leads to the road. Turn left on the metalled road and go down the hill into the pretty village of Loddington, where you will see Loddington Hall straight ahead of you. Follow the road round to the right and then turn left to East Norton. At the bottom of the hill take the right-hand fork into a dry ford, marked bridleway, and follow this track through the metal gate and on down to the deserted farm buildings at Loddington Mill. Go through a second ford and then bear left to follow the line of the brook for a little way before swinging south across an arable field to a gate into a grass field. Ride across this field and exit by the next gate on to the road (GR.782005), with East Norton Hall on your left. *If conditions are very wet, it is recommended that you proceed direct from Loddington to East Norton along the small, quiet road which has excellent verges.* **Turn left to East Norton and ride straight along the old road until it meets the A47 (GR.789002) where you will find a crossing place marked with a horseshoe.** *CAUTION - visibility is limited to your left, but you can see far enough to see a clear space in the traffic.*

Cross the road and follow the byway past a large barn to meet the metalled road. Carry straight on for 200 yards to turn left on to a stony track before the road descends steeply. Follow this track in an easterly direction until you come to a gate into a large grass field. Staying on top of the hill, and keeping near to the fence, bear right after the Trig. point; do not go through the gate which is dead ahead. Continue until you eventually reach a wooden farm gate leading into a lane where you will recognise Fearn Farm and your starting point, just below you along the lane.

71

TRAIL
19

A 17 MILE CIRCULAR TRAIL (CLOCKWISE)

Ordnance Survey Maps:
Pathfinder: 915, 916, 936 & 937
Landranger: 140

Parking & Starting Point:
You may park on the large car park at the Bath Hotel at Shearsby(GR.621902)but as a matter of courtesy, please telephone (0533) 478202, beforehand.

Route Information: *There are a number of short cuts not mentioned in the text but that are obvious from the map. This part of Leicestershire is pleasantly rural and the route consists of bridleways, grass and other tracks with some minor metalled road work. There are no major road crossings.*

Route Description:

Ride from The Bath Hotel car park and turn right. Continue for about 0.25 miles up the road and turn right at the bridleway sign opposite the T-junction (GR.625095) to Shearsby. The bridleway goes across fields to the west side of Knaptoft House Farm and then it goes diagonally south-east to the east side of the fishponds. Continue across fields leaving Knaptoft Grange to the west and go across the driveway to Knaptoft Grange before joining a track to ride across grass fields going west from Warren Farm (GR.629880). This track is across grass fields to begin with and then it goes through overgrown hedges to both sides of the track and through a gate before joining the Bruntingthorpe-Walton road. *CARE*

should be taken on entering the road as visibility is limited.

Turn left onto the road and continue until you reach the outskirts of Walton village. Take the first turning left down Park Lane and follow the road round to rejoin the main village street by the Dog & Gun Public House. Turn left onto the road and continue down the road to the village of Kimcote. On entering Kimcote village take the first turning left into Poultney Lane (GR.585865), just before the church and continue along the lane until you reach a gate with a bridleway sign, towards Walcote. Follow the bridleway, keeping the fence to the left until you reach Great Poultney Farm which is on your left. The bridleway continues in the same direction across an arable field and finally goes into a small, humpy grass field which has a handgate. Ride through and out onto the lane between Gilmorton and Walcote (GR.571844).

The route then turns right, going north, and goes up the lane to Gilmorton again. After about 1.25 miles the route joins the Kimcote to Lutterworth road (GR.572865). Riders should turn left here where it is signposted Lutterworth. After about 300 yards turn right at the signpost for Gilmorton. Ride on into the village. Passing The Talbot Public House continue up to the T-junction where you keep The Crown Public House on the right-hand side. Turn right, and then immediately left, where it is signposted Peatling Parva. In about

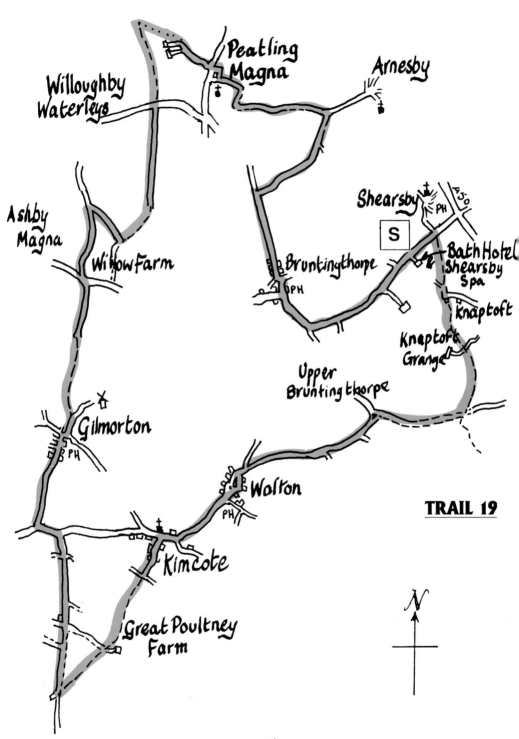

Willoughby
Waterleys

Peatling
Magna

Arnesby

Ashby
Magna

Shearsby

PH

A50

S

Willow Farm

Bruntingthorpe

PH

Bath Hotel
Shearsby
Spa

Knaptoft

Knaptoft
Grange

Upper
Bruntingthorpe

Gilmorton

PH

Walton

PH

TRAIL 19

Kimcote

Great Poultney
Farm

N

200 yards bear left going through a metal gate and onto a track (GR.573881) and follow the track northwards. This track is mainly grass, following between hedges and it continues for about 1.25 miles towards Willow Farm.

When you come to the Peatling Parva to Ashby Magna road, riders should turn left and then go immediately right up a track, leaving Willow Farm to the right. After following the track for just over a mile, the route turns sharp right (GR.577909) and goes south-east towards the left-hand corner of a small wood where it turns sharp left and continues up another track for about 1.50 miles before crossing the Peatling Magna-Willoughby Waterleys road (GR.586923). *Parts of this track are rutted and muddy and care should be taken. Later on the track becomes hard with a loose gritty surface.*

The route continues over the road and through a new metal gate and along the side of an arable field leaving the hedgerow to the left. *This is not marked on your Ordnance Survey maps.* At the end of this field the route follows a grass track between two hedges. After riding for approximately 0.75 miles the route turns right onto another track which continues on leaving Peatling Lodge Farm to the right and takes you to eventually join the Countesthorpe-Peatling Magna road on the north side of Peatling Magna. *Most of the last part of this track has a firm surface. In the village you will find The Cock Inn and also a telephone box.*

On entering Peatling Magna turn right and then almost immediately left down School Lane. Follow this lane round until it joins the Peatling Magna-Arnesby lane where your route turns left. You will now be riding along a gated road, part of it unfenced, with adjacent old pasture until it joins the Arnesby-Bruntingthorpe road by some elaborate new buildings where you turn right (GR.610921). The route continues on this lane until joining the Bruntingthorpe-Peatling Magna road (GR.600910) where riders should turn left and follow the signpost for Bruntingthorpe. Ride through the village of Bruntingthorpe.

At the southern edge of the village there is a road junction to the right, but your route continues bearing left, signposted to Shearsby. After about 0.50 miles the road turns sharp left at the entrance to Bruntingthorpe Airfield and continues past the T-junction to Walton, down the hill past the entrance to Knaptoft House Farm and so back to your starting point at the Bath Hotel. *CARE is needed on the last piece of road as it is used by vehicles from Bruntingthorpe Airfield.*

Thatched Cottage at Peatling Parva.

THE BRITISH HORSE SOCIETY

The British Horse Society was founded in 1947 when two separate equestrian bodies - The National Horse Association and the Institute of the Horse and Pony Club - decided to join forces and work together for the good of both horse and rider.

It is a marriage that has proved to be a great success and the British Horse Society has steadily increased its membership from just 4000 in the late 1960's to over 60,000 in the 1990's.

By becoming members of the British Horse Society, horse lovers know they are joining a body of people with a shared interest in the horse. Members can be sure that they are contributing to the work of an equine charity with a primary aim to improve the standards of care for horses and ponies. Welfare is not only about the rescuing of horses in distress (which we do); it is also about acting to prevent abuse in the first place. There are many means to achieving this: by teaching and advising, by looking to the horse's well-being and safety, by providing off-road riding, by encouraging high standards in all equestrian establishments, and fighting for the horse's case with government and in Europe.

The British Horse Society works tirelessly towards these aims thanks to the work of its officials at Stoneleigh and its army of dedicated volunteers out in the field.

Membership benefits the horse lover as well as the horse; the Society can offer something to all equestrians, whether they are weekend riders, interested spectators or keen competitors. The benefits include free Third Party Public Liability and Personal Accident insurance, free legal advice, free publications, reductions to British Horse Society events, special facilities at the major shows, and free advice and information on any equine query.

Largely financed by its membership subscriptions, the Society welcomes the support of all horse lovers. If you are thinking of joining the Society and would like to find out more about our work, please contact the Membership Department at the following address:

The British Horse Society
British Equestrian Centre
Stoneleigh Park
Kenilworth
Warwickshire
CV8 2LR
(Telephone: 0203 696697)
Registered Charity No. 210504